COLORING BOOKS FOR ADULTS RELAXATION

Mindfulness

SWEAR WORD, MANDALA
FLOWER AND DOODLE DESIGNS

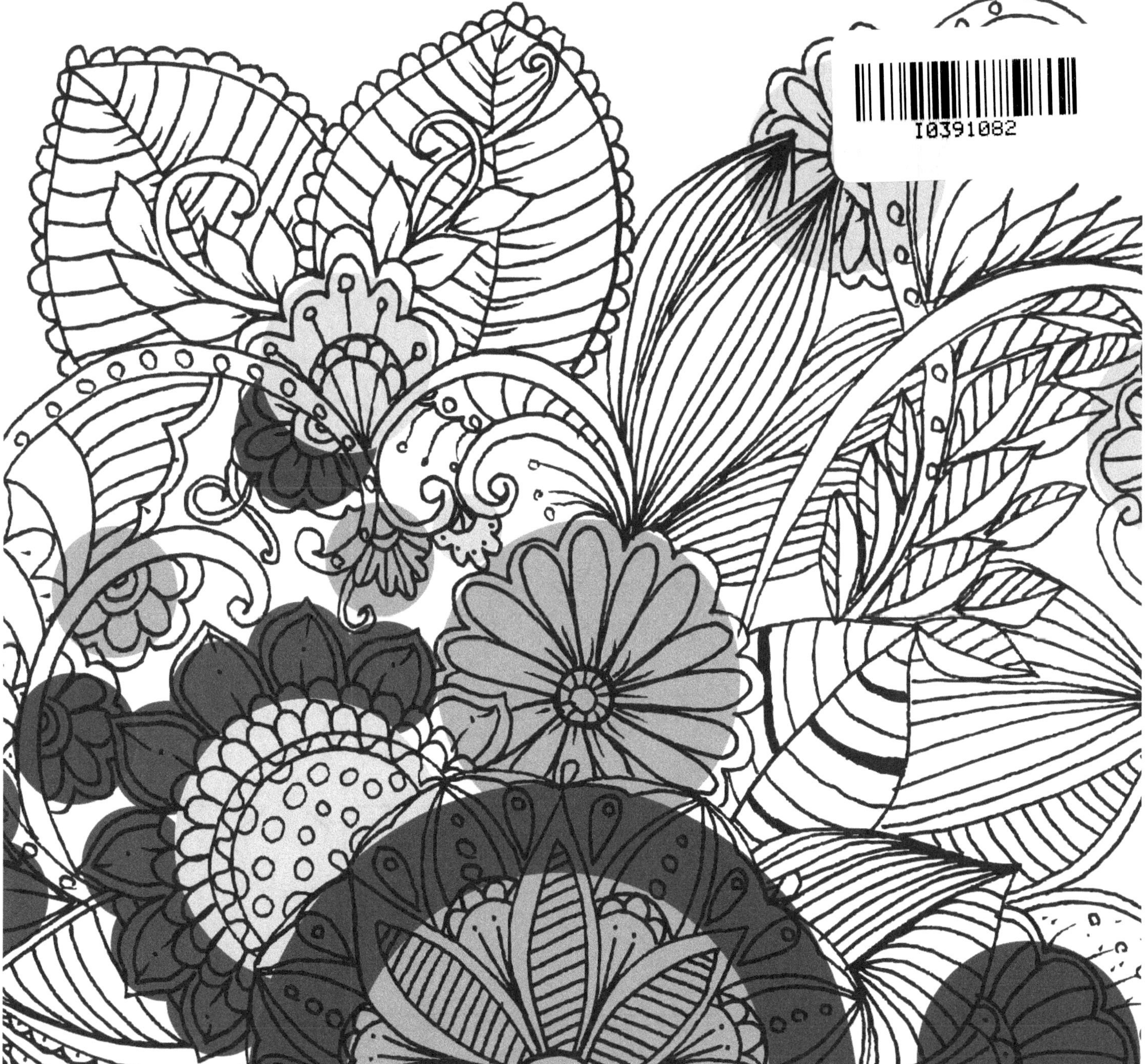

TEST YOUR COLOR

TEST YOUR COLOR

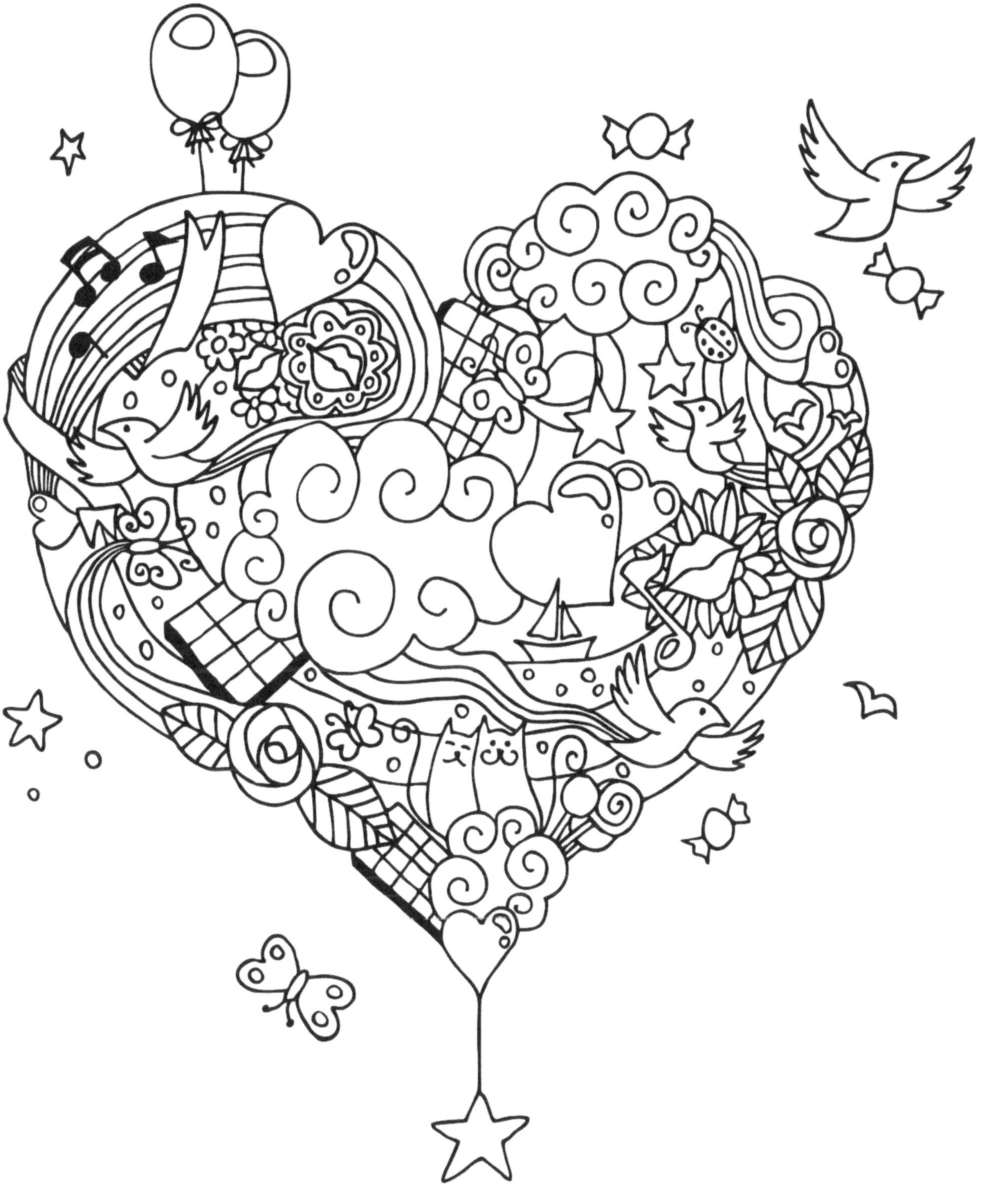

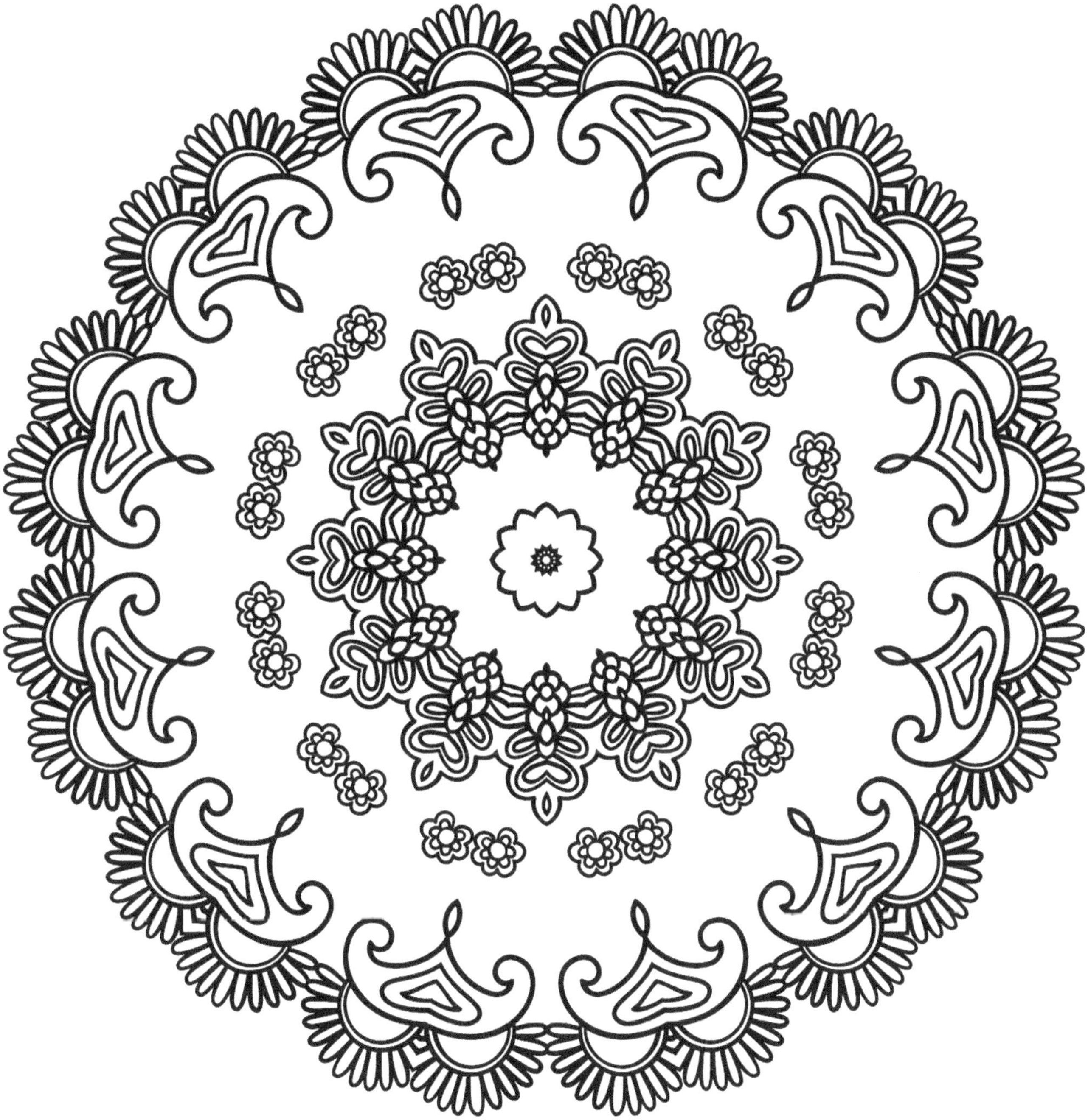

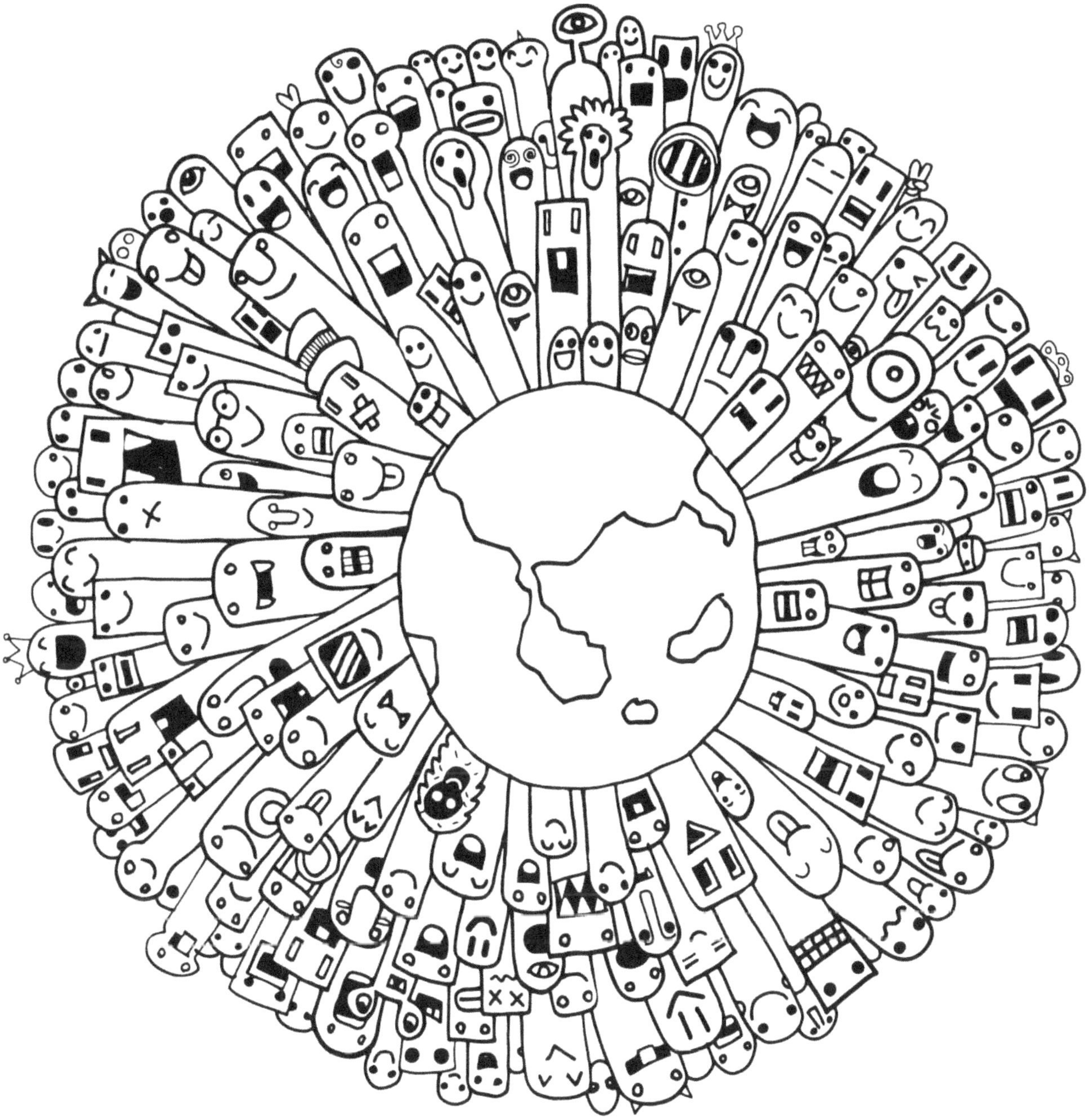

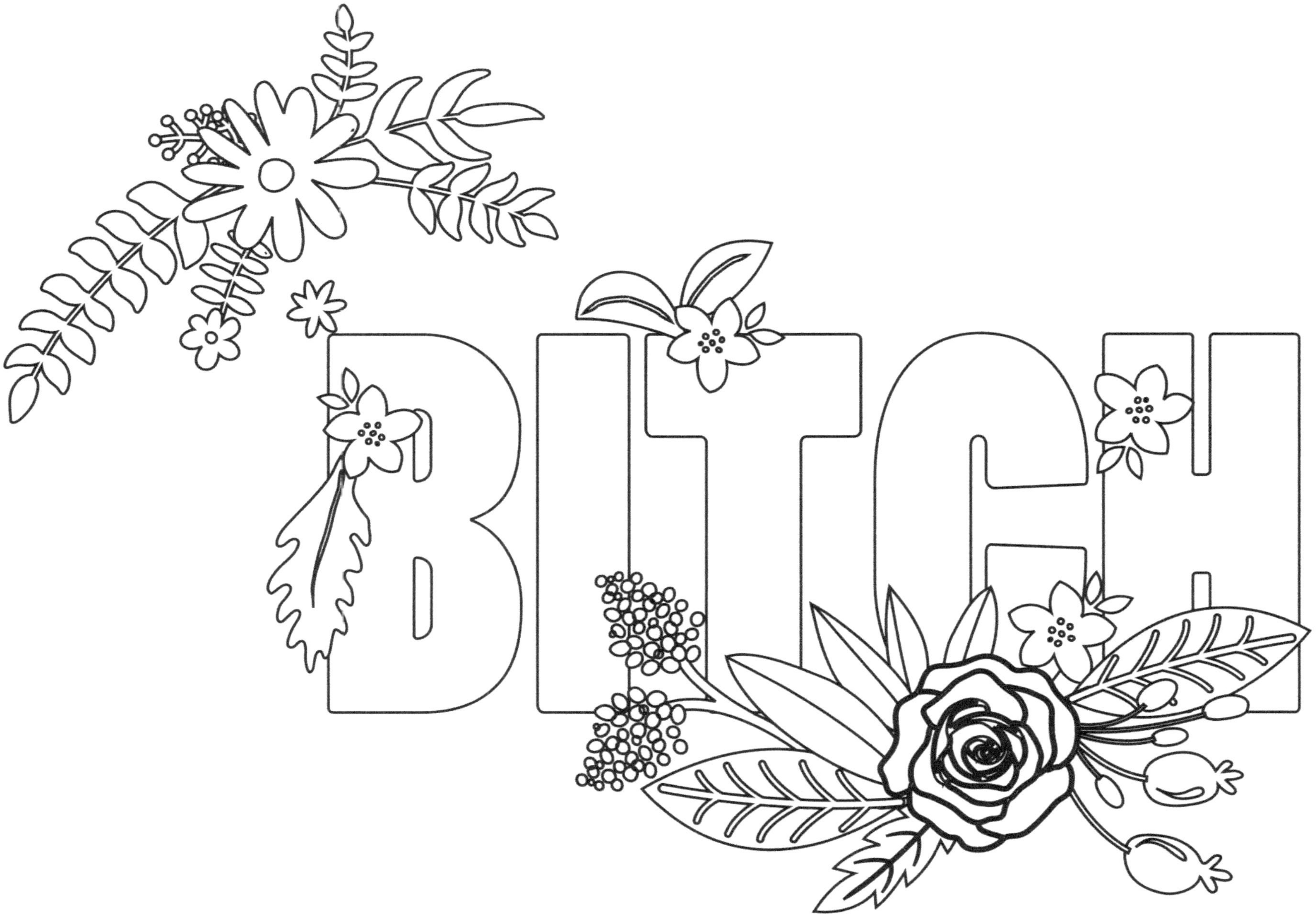
BITCH

BULLSHIT

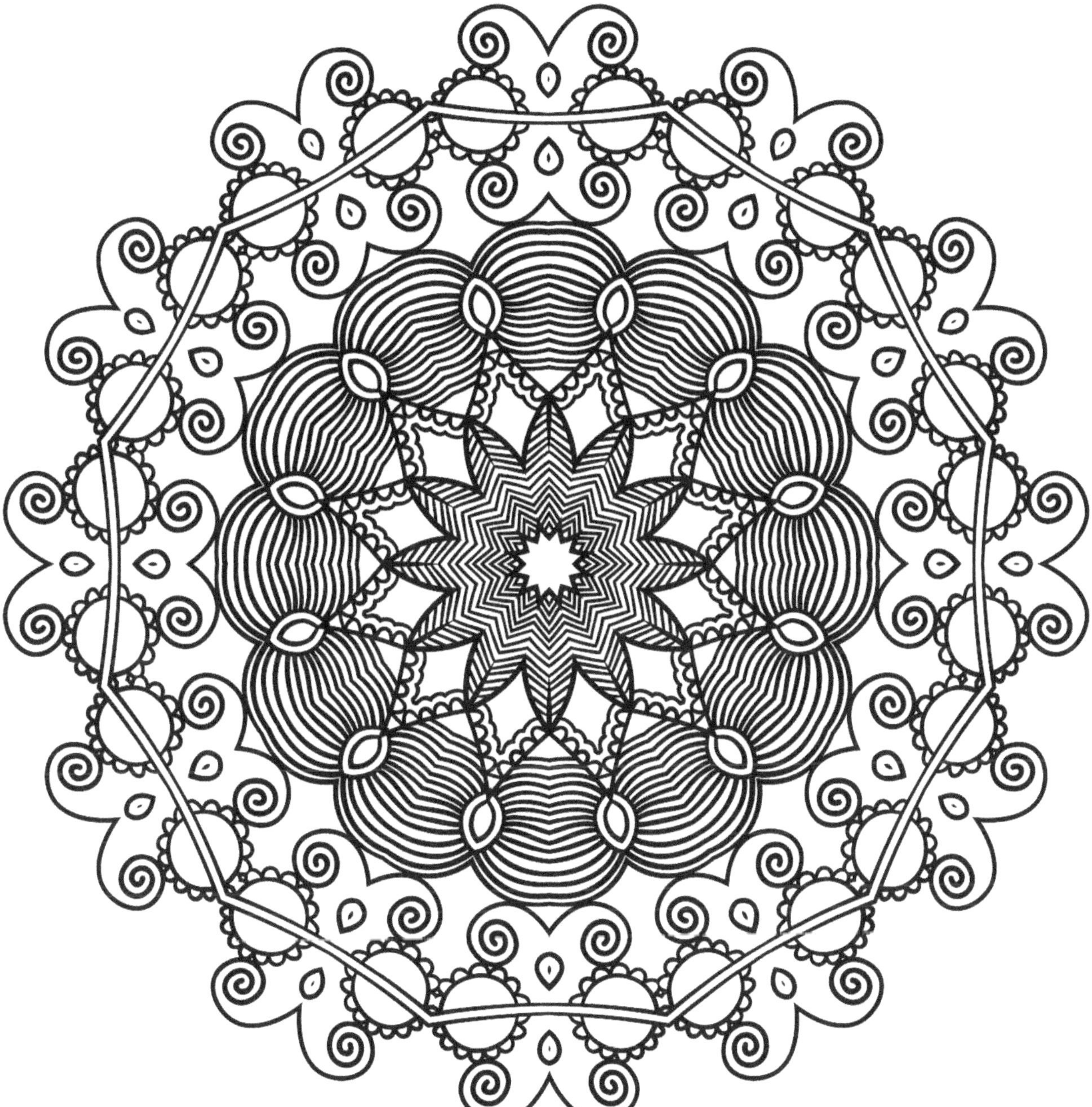

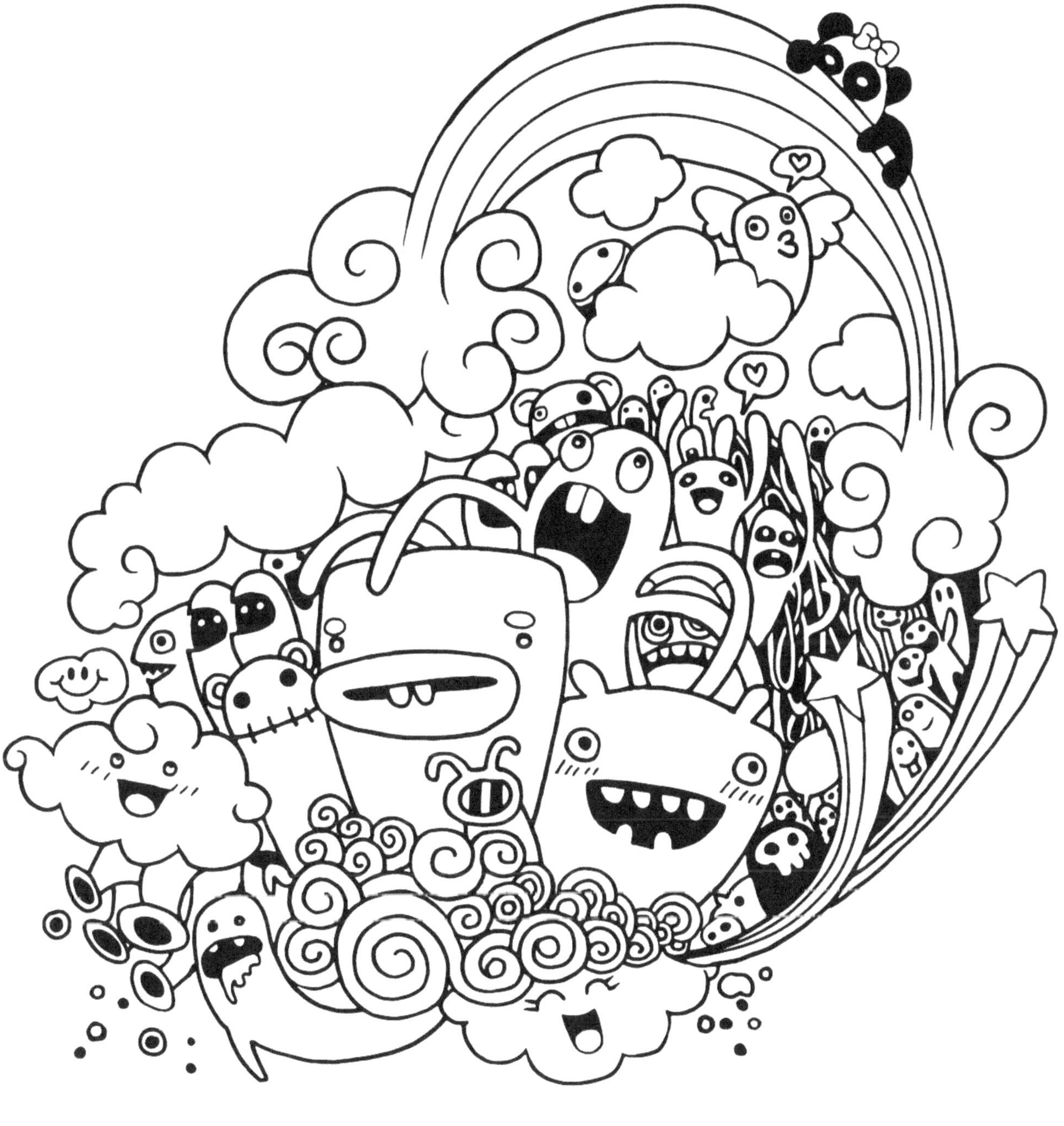

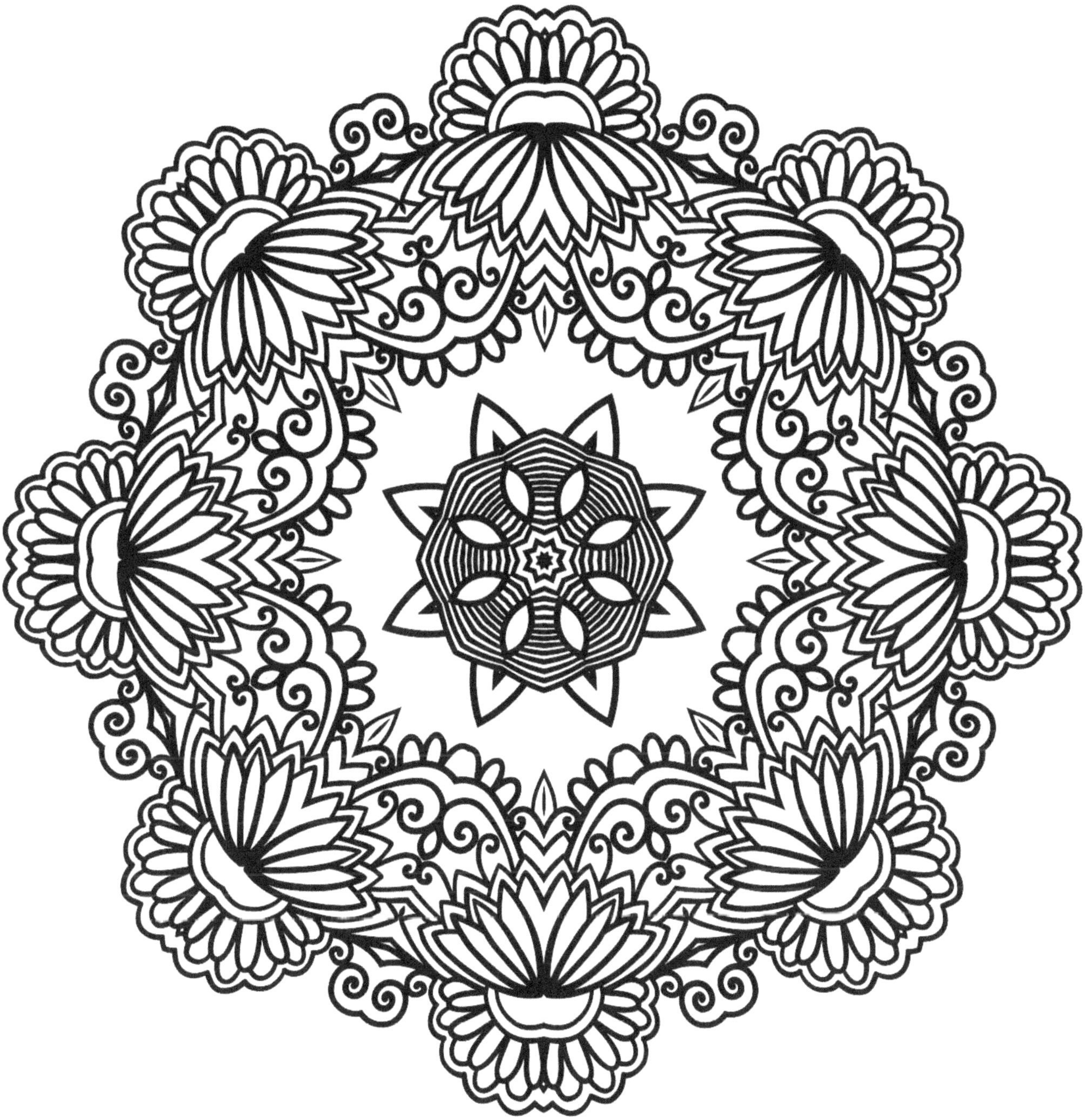

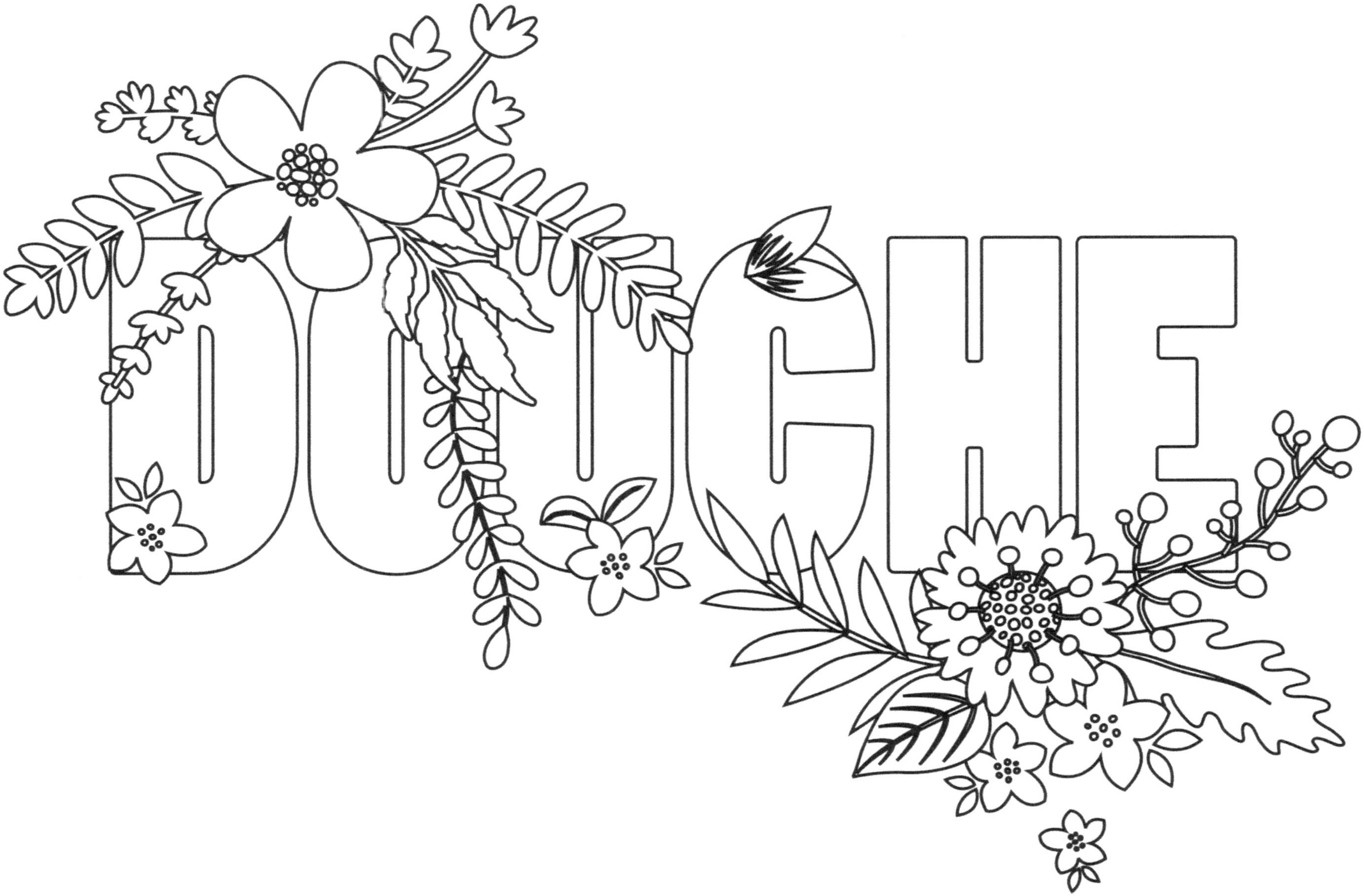
DOUCHE

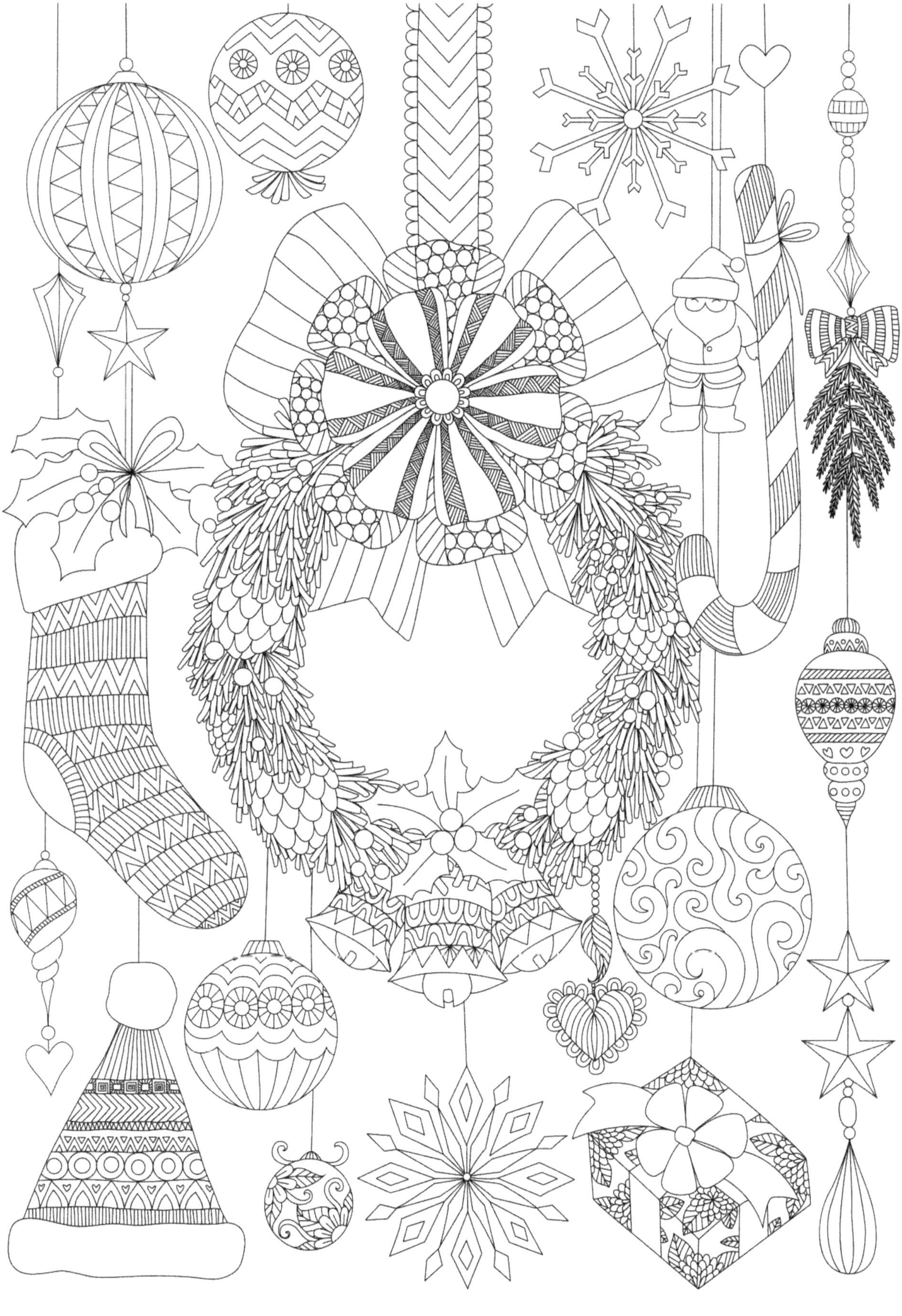

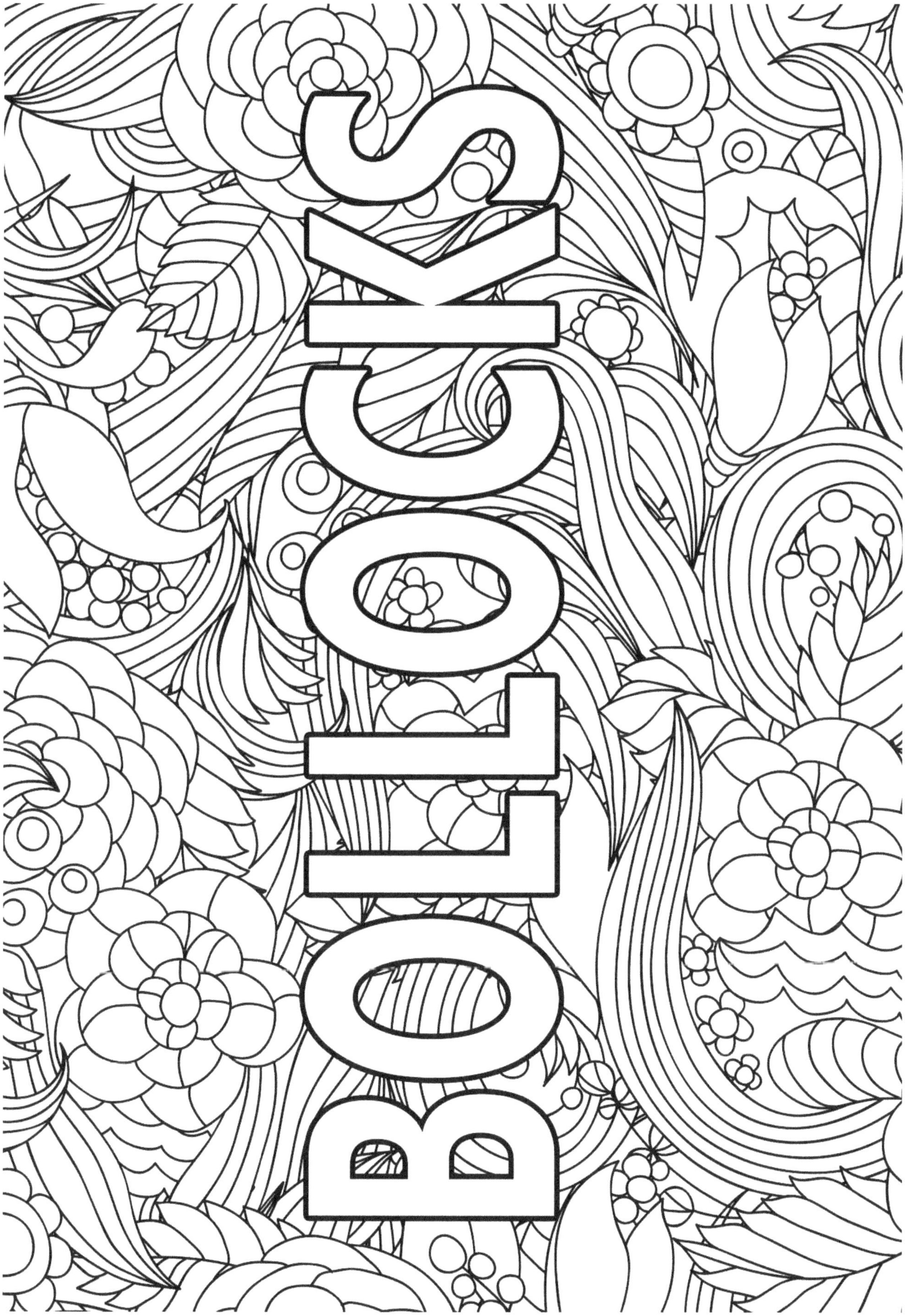
BOLLOCKS

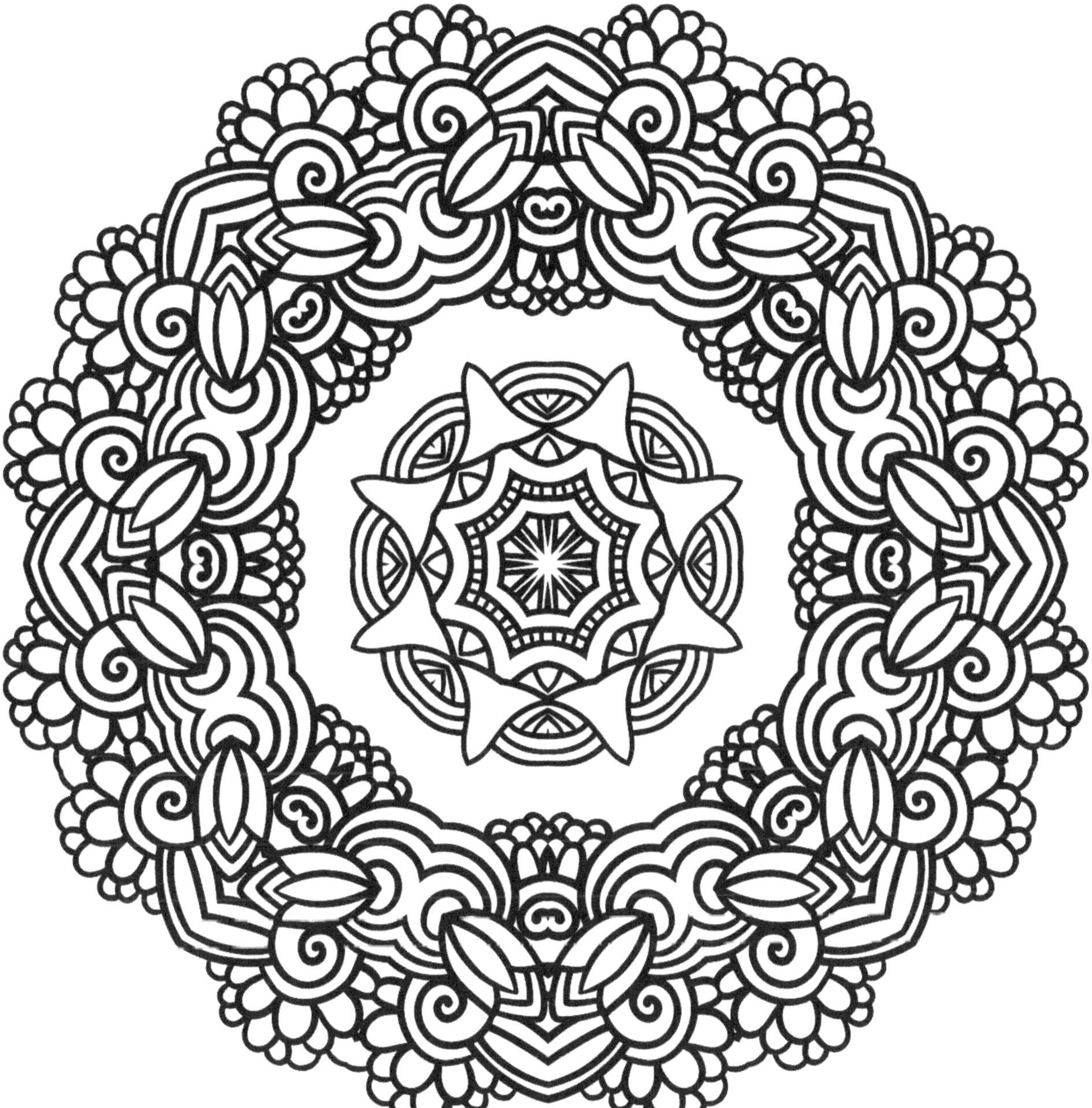

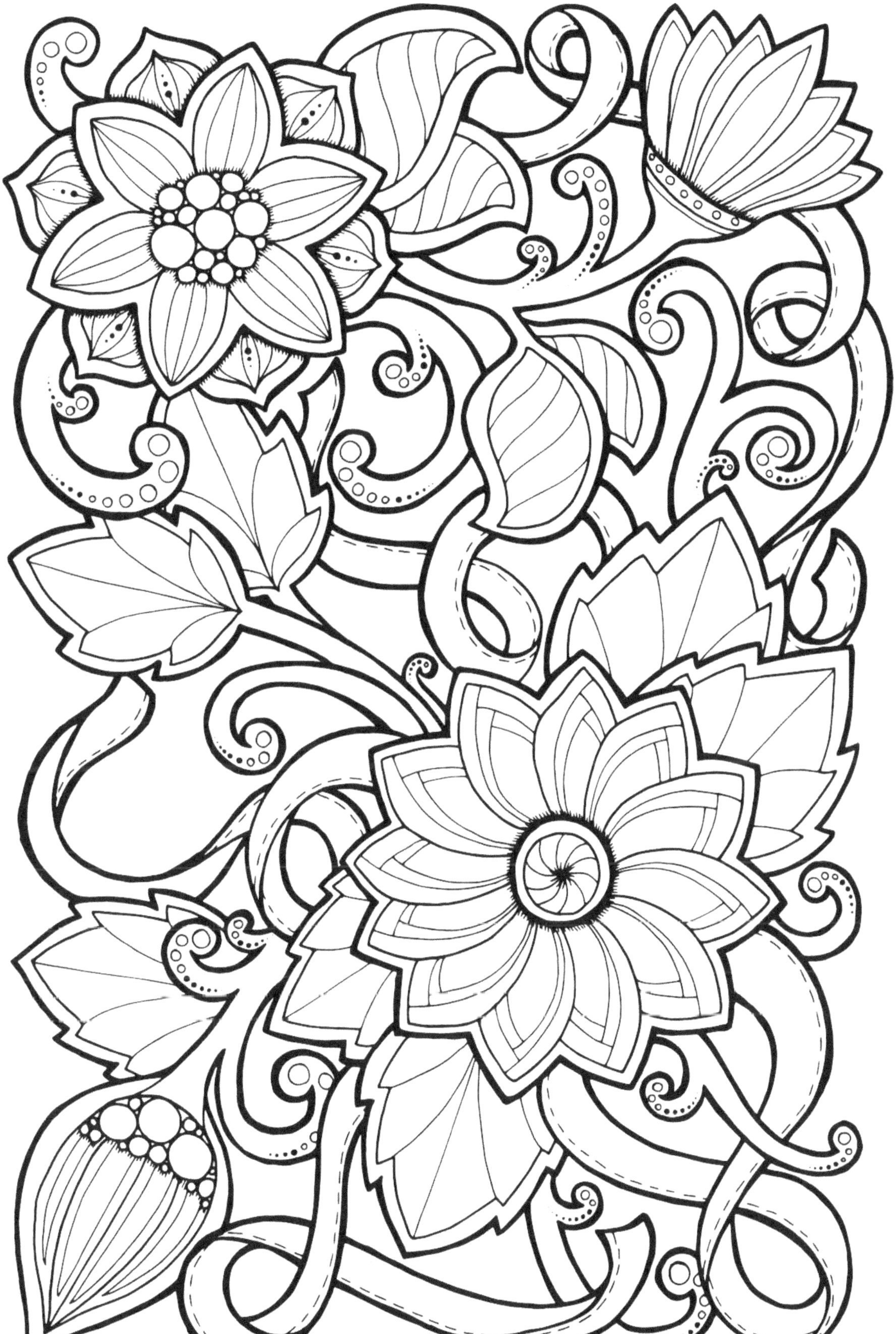

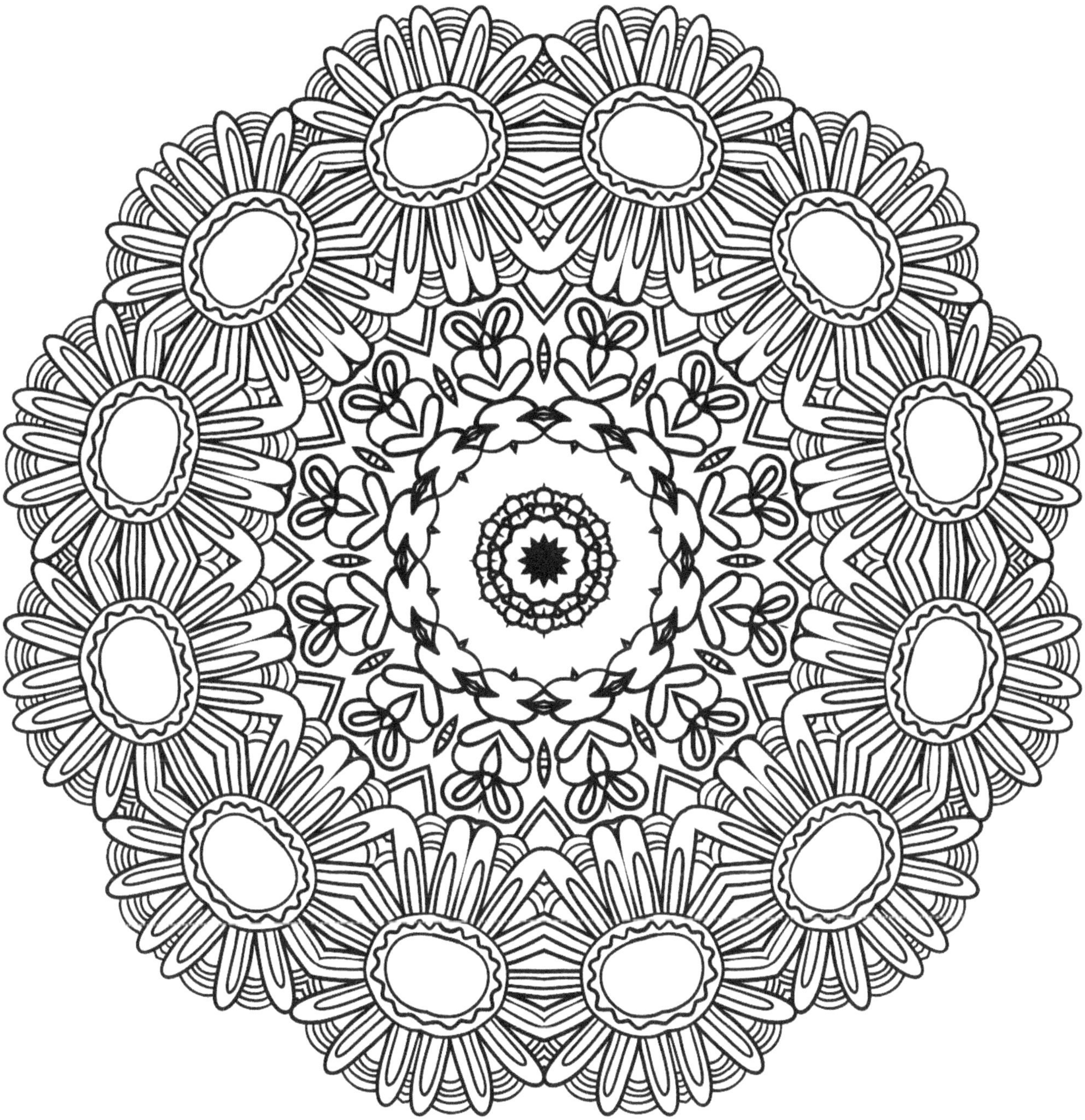

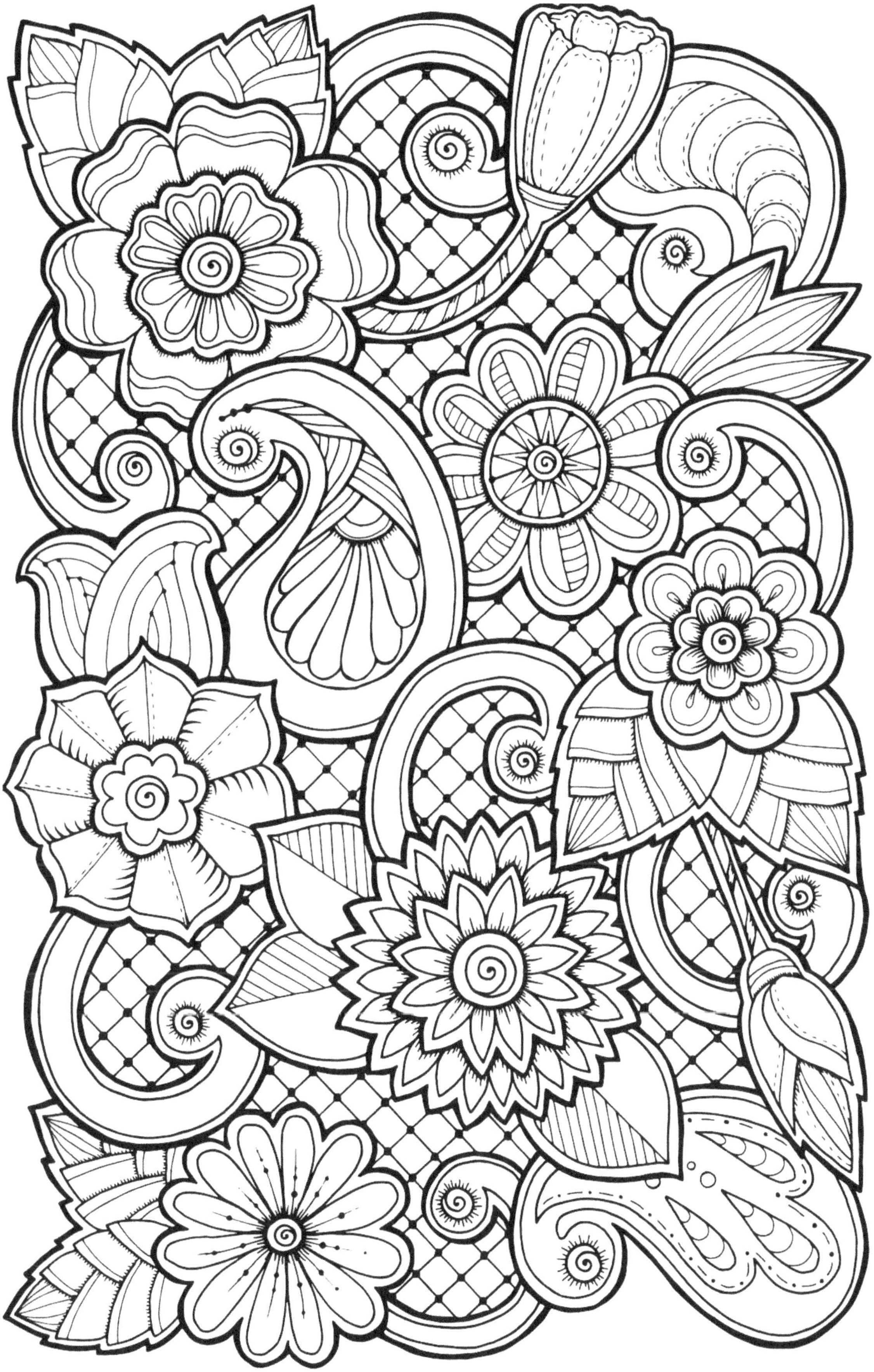

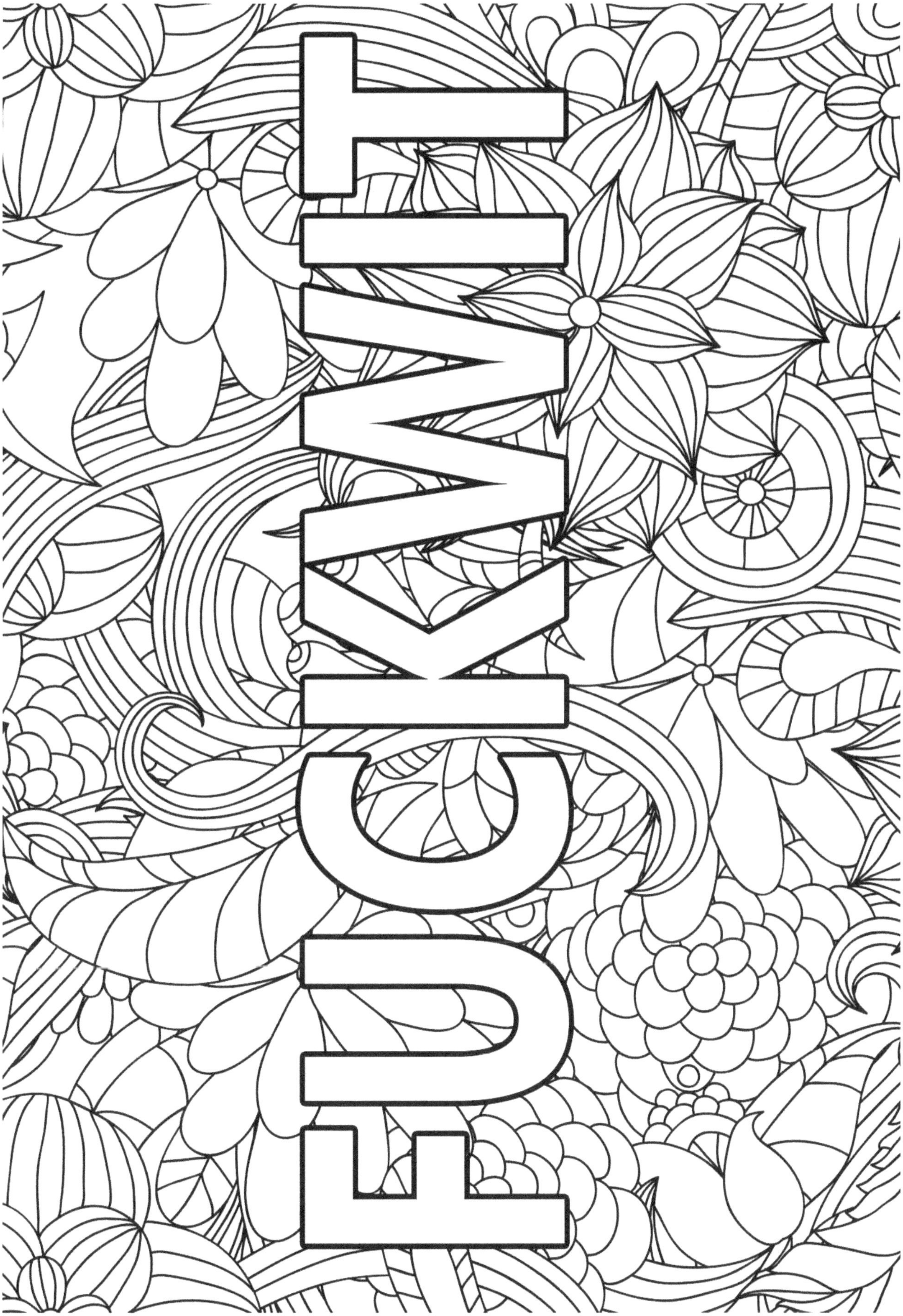
FUCKIT

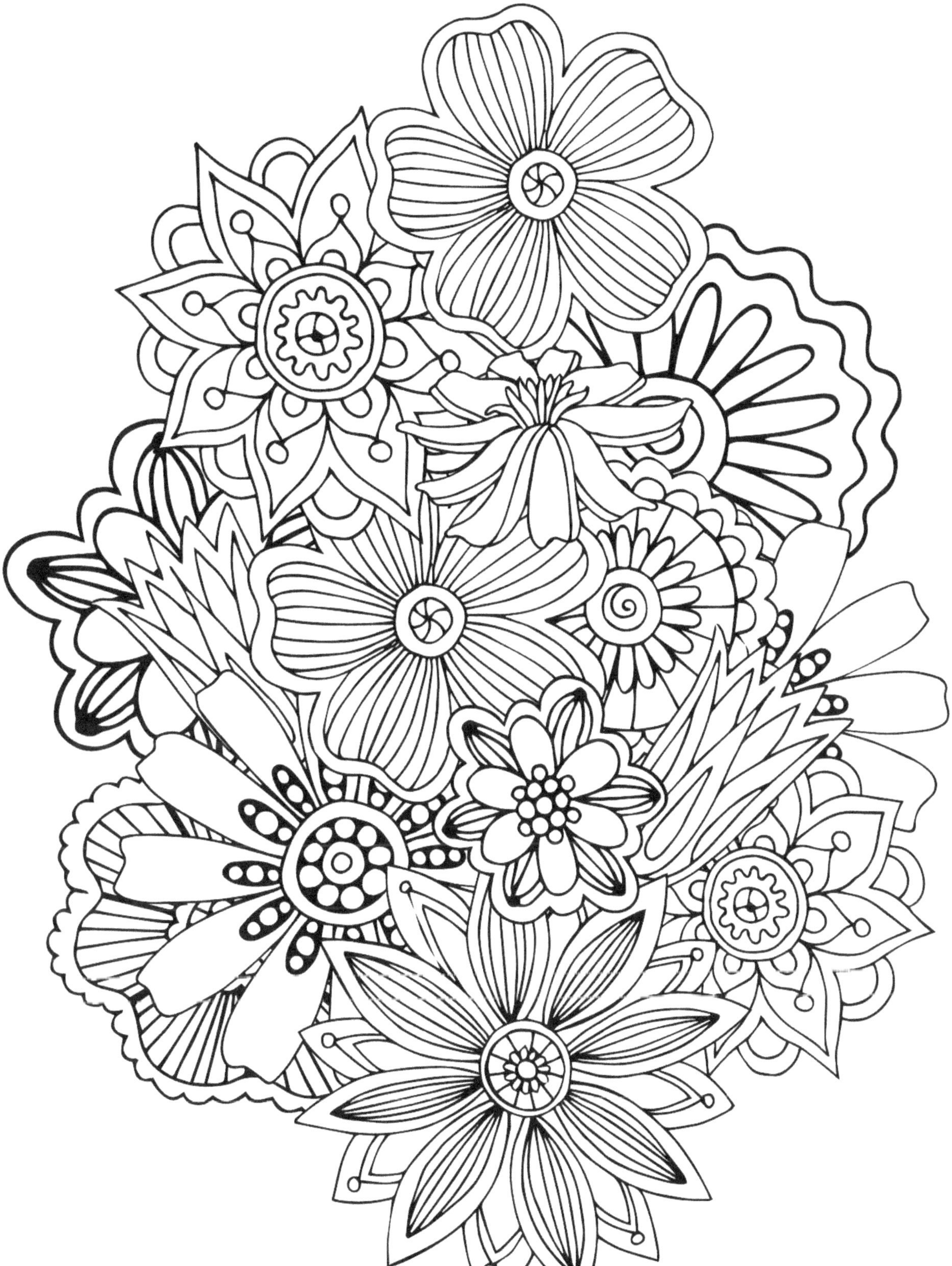

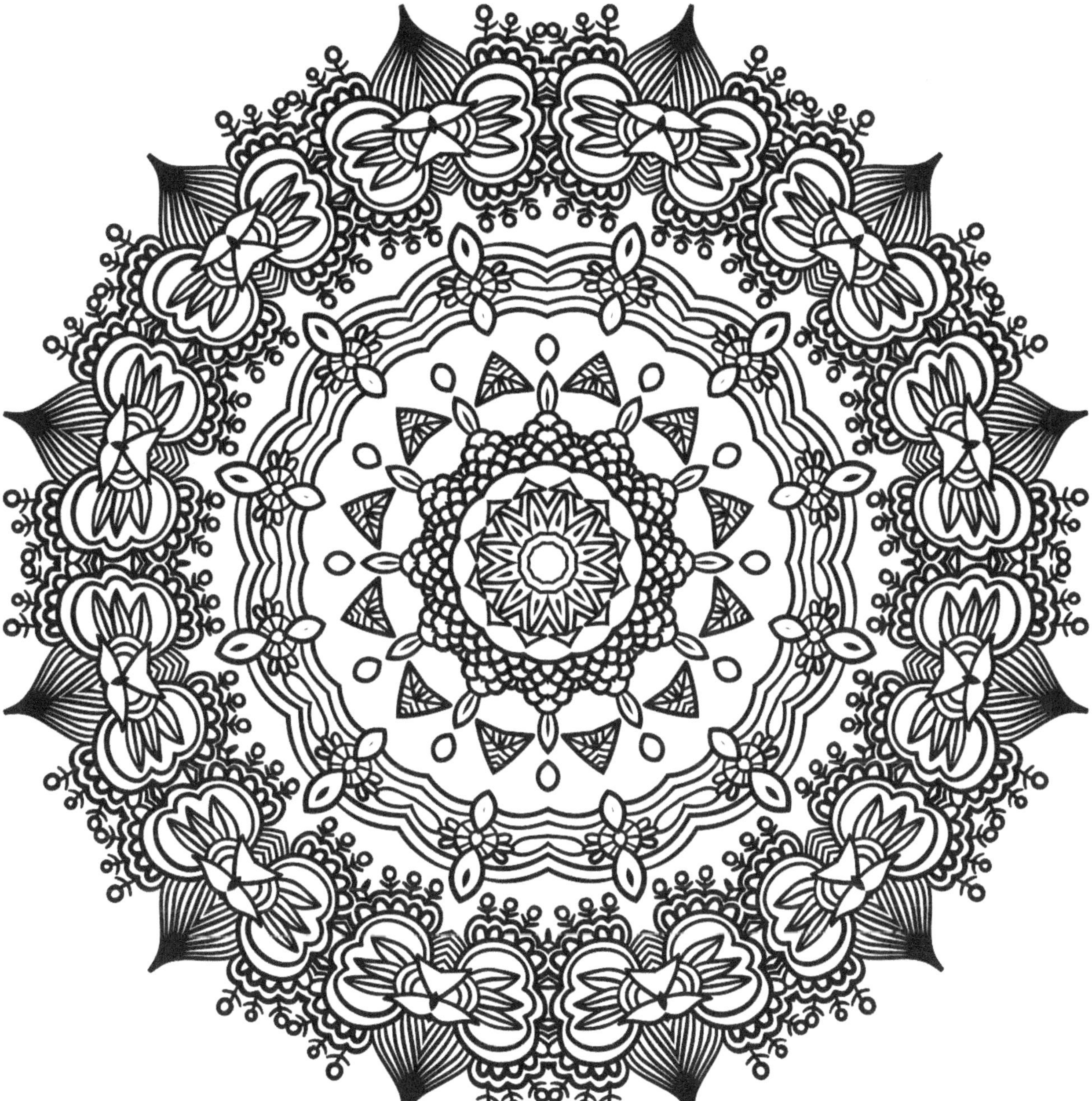

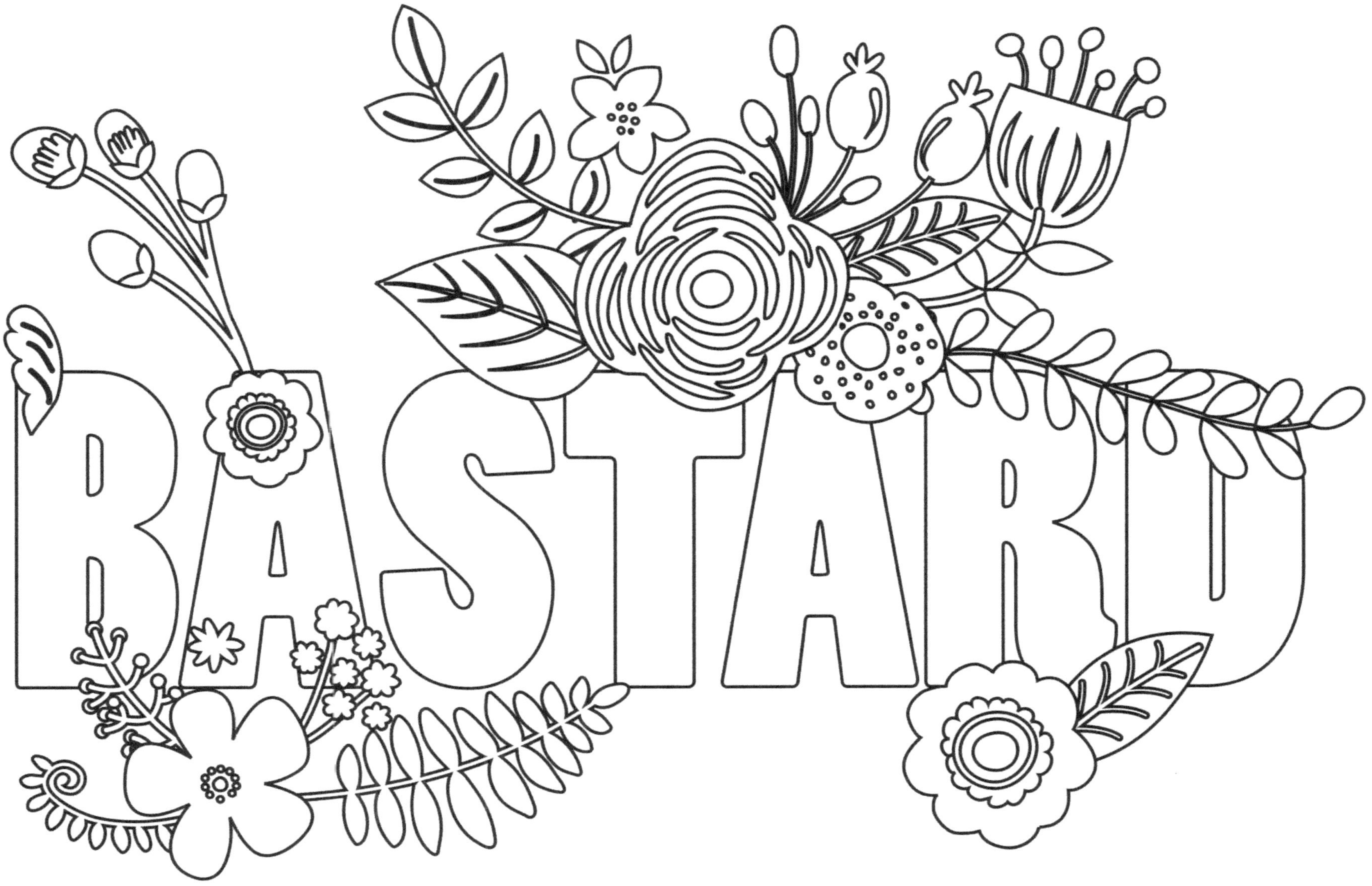
BASTARD

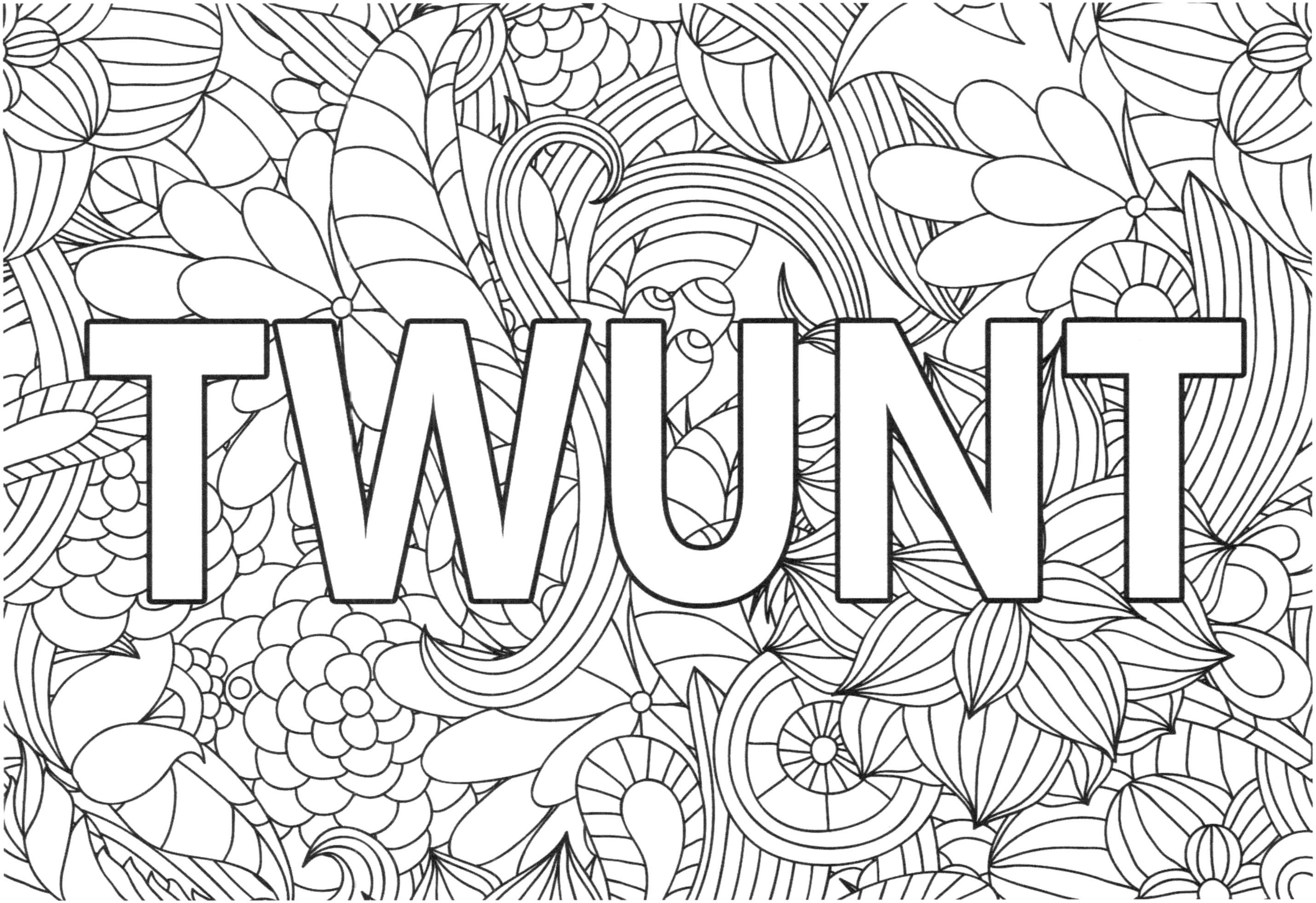
TWUNT

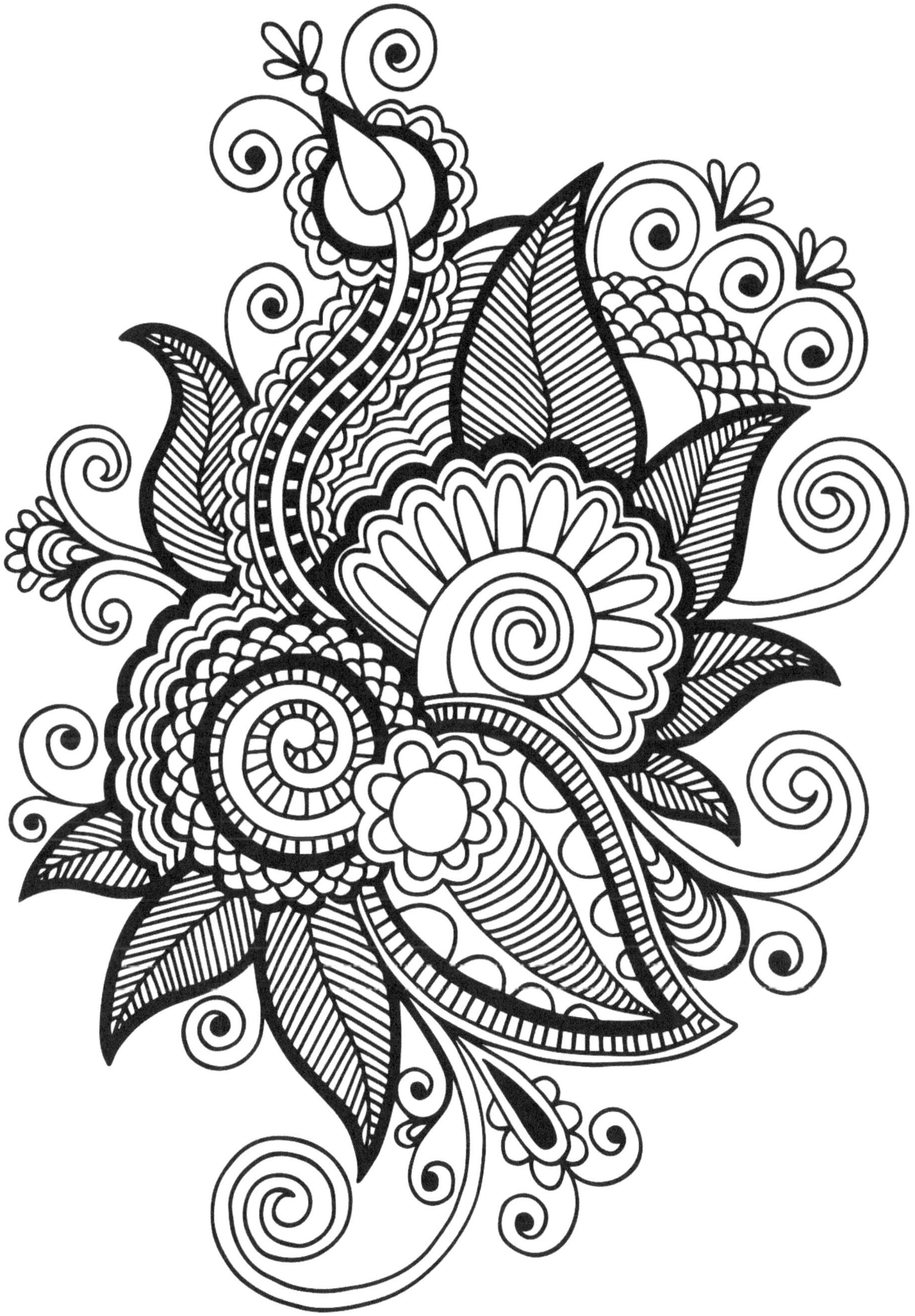

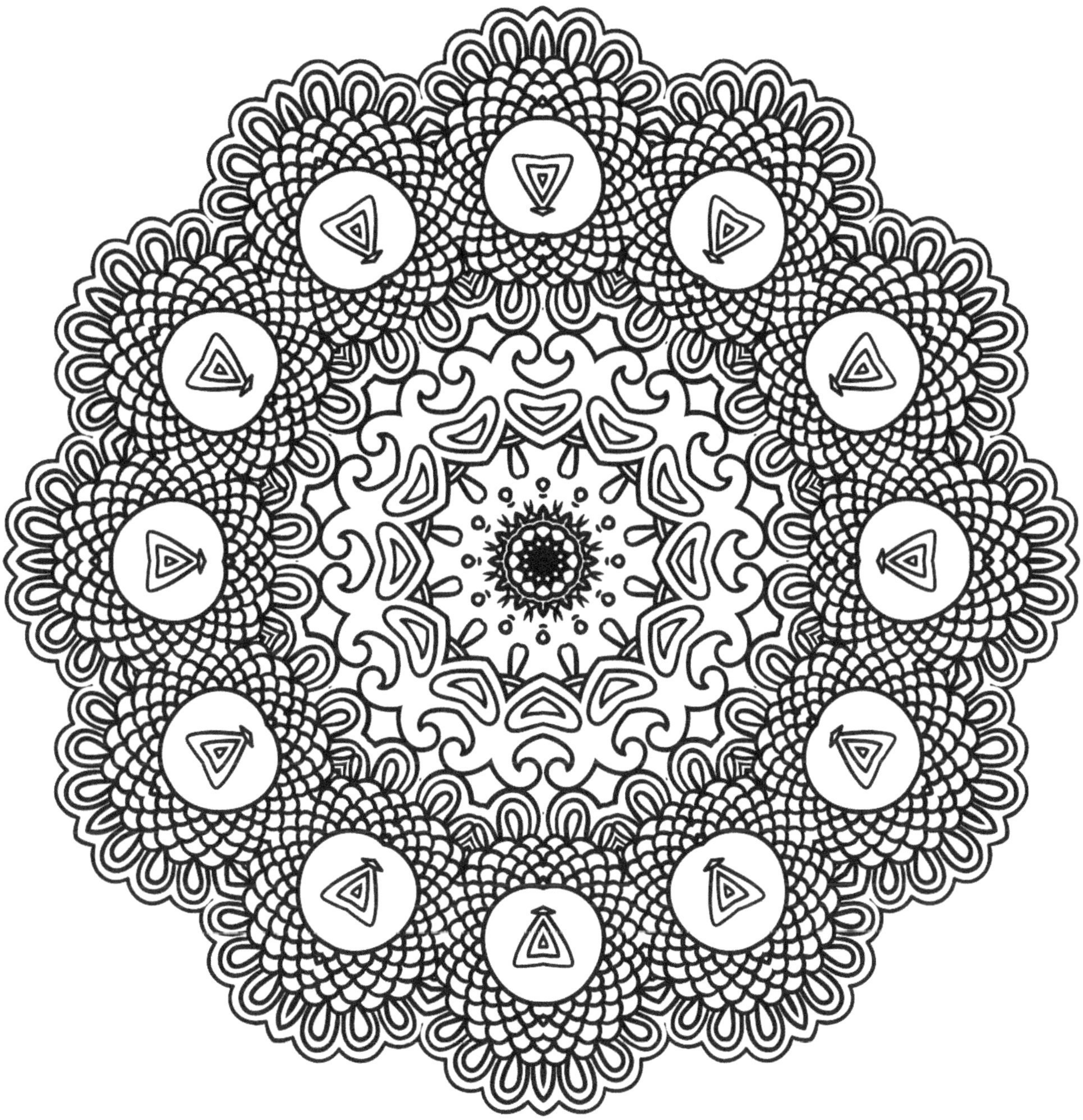

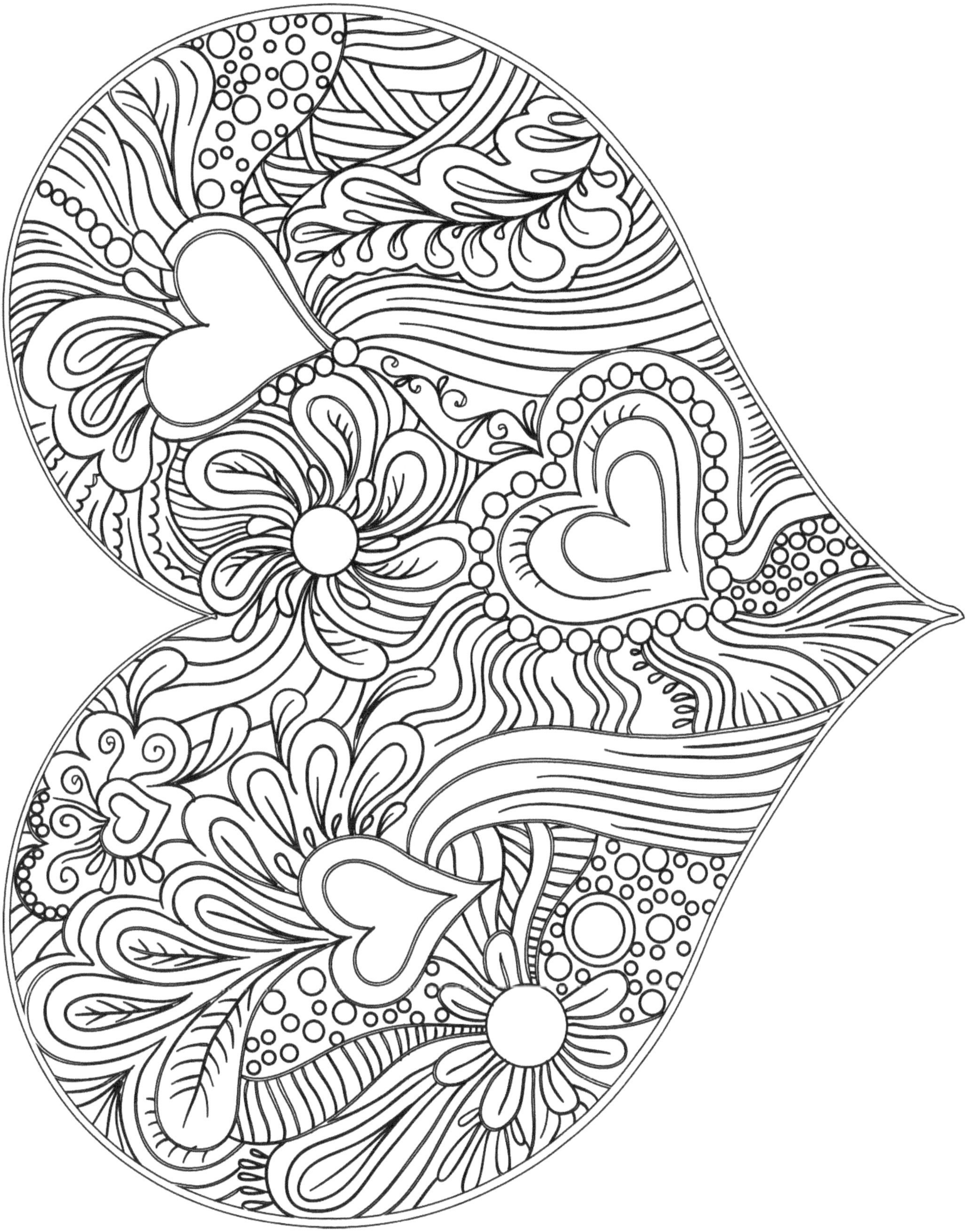

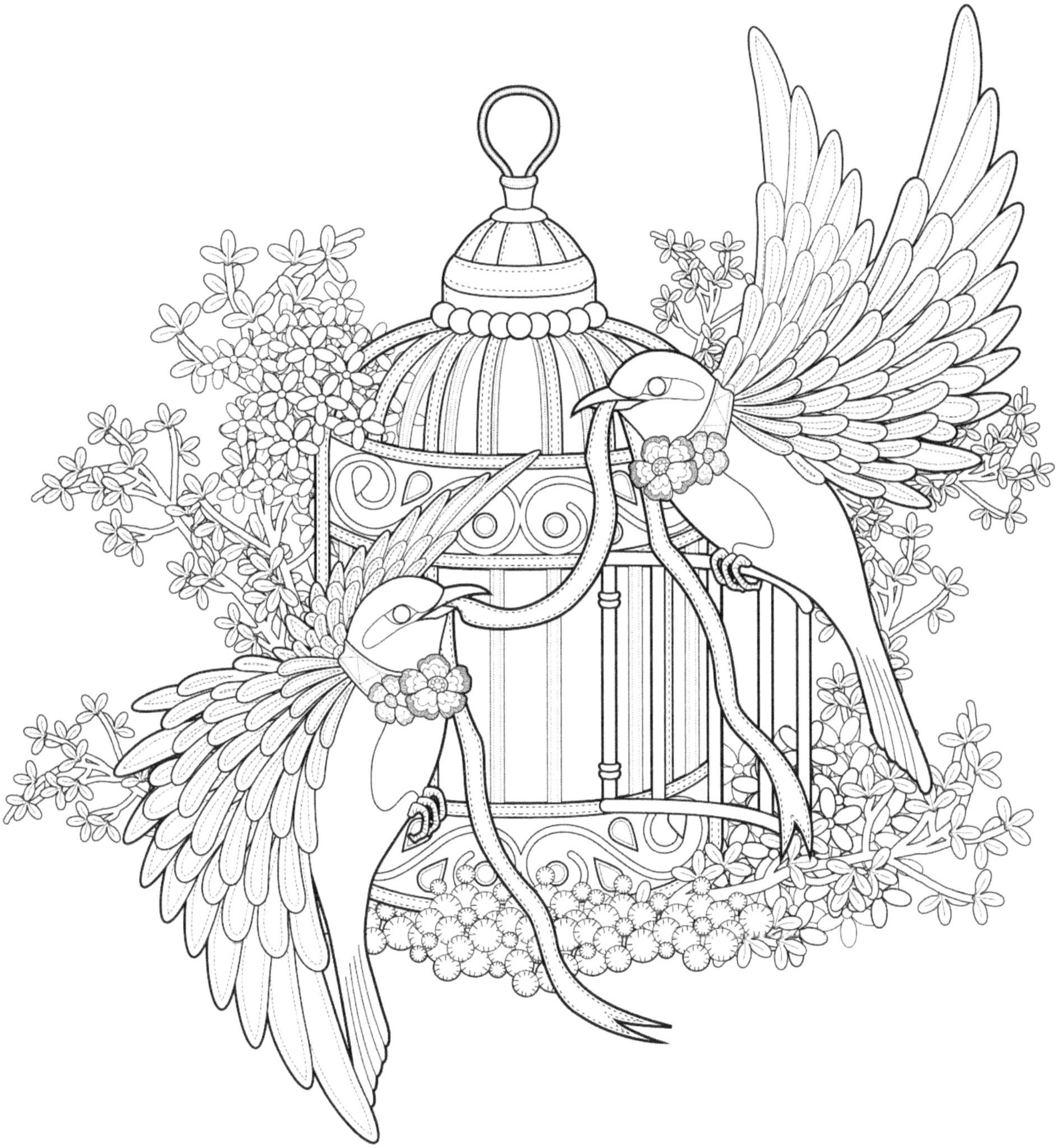

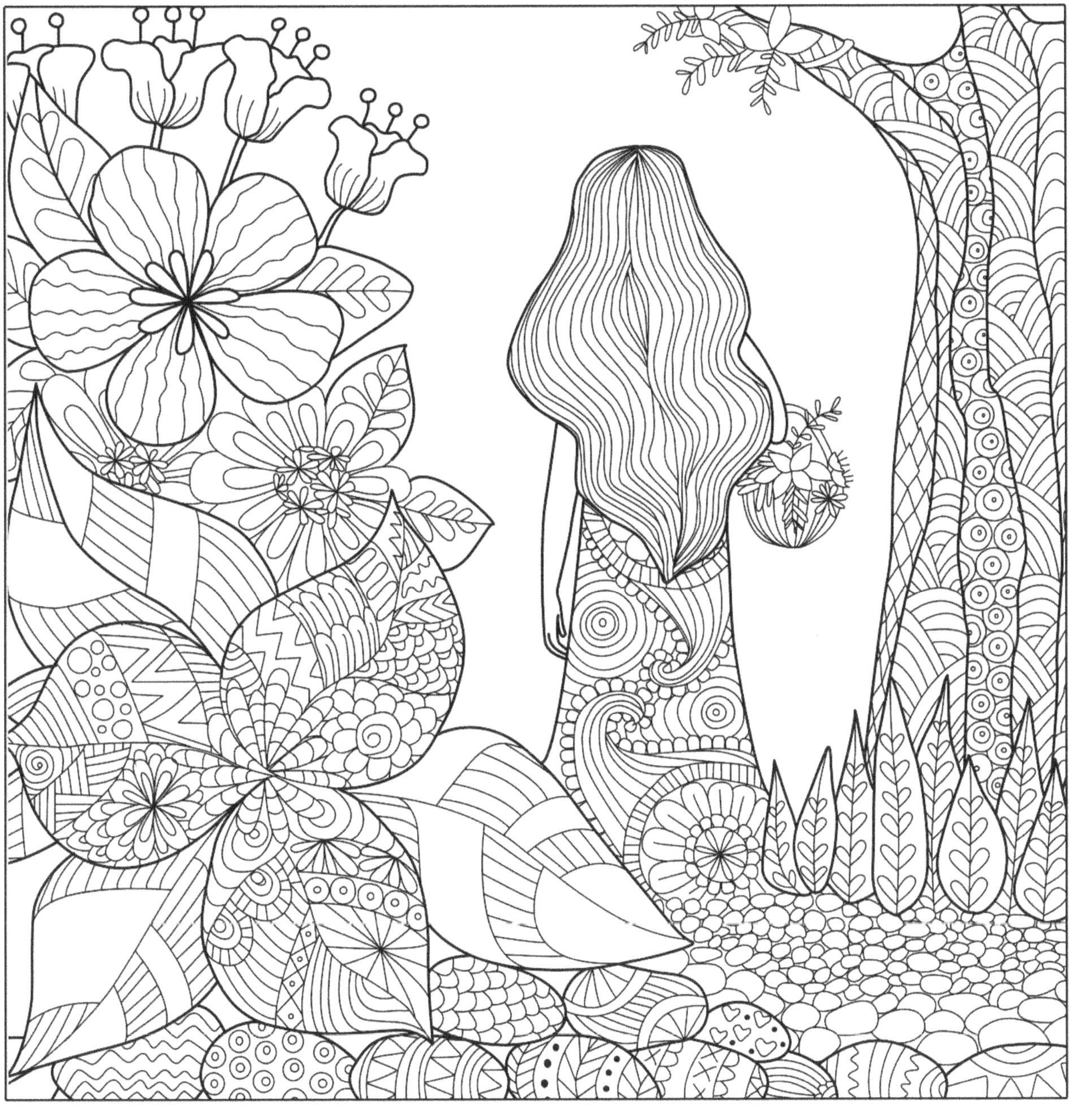

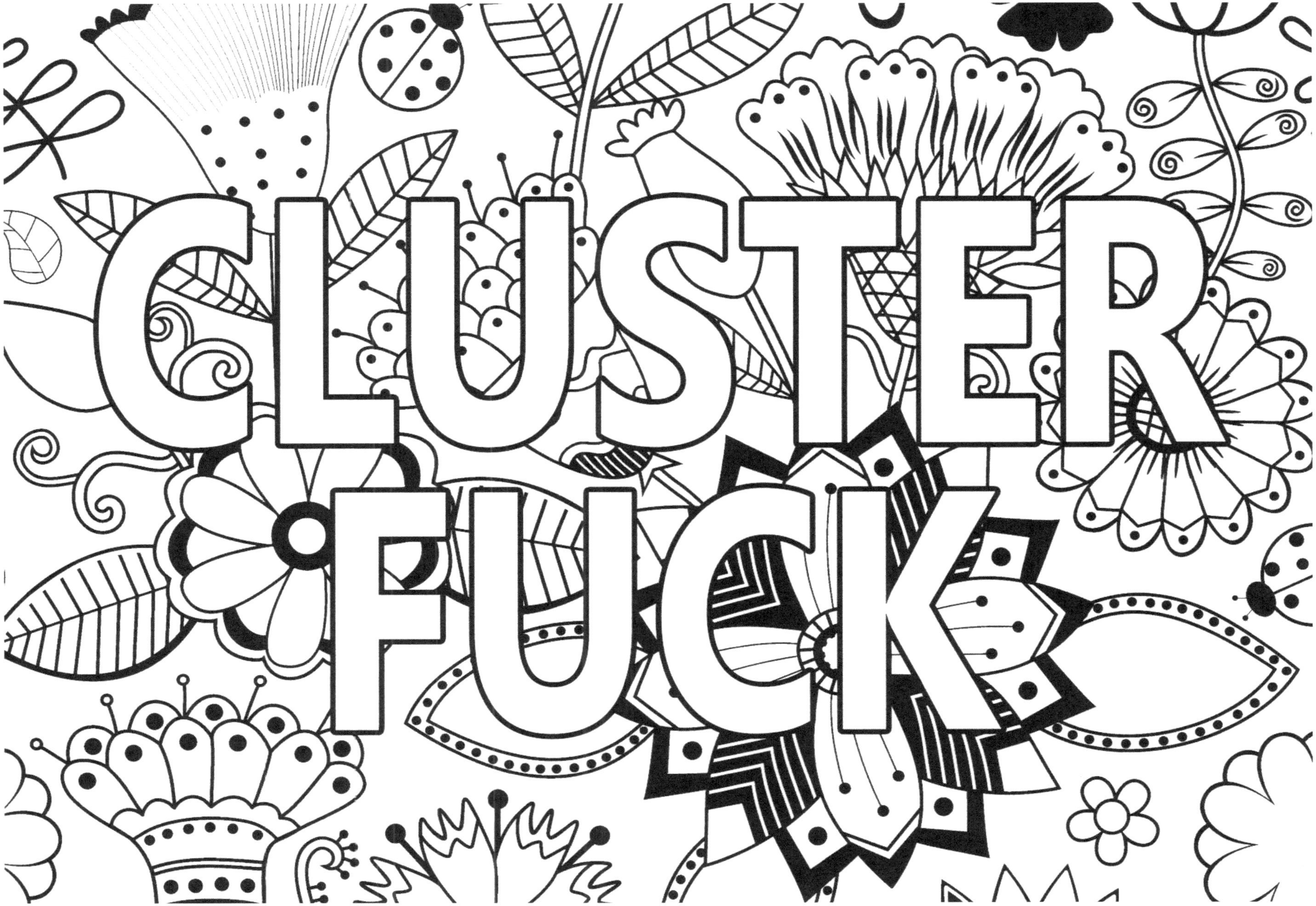
CLUSTER
FUCK

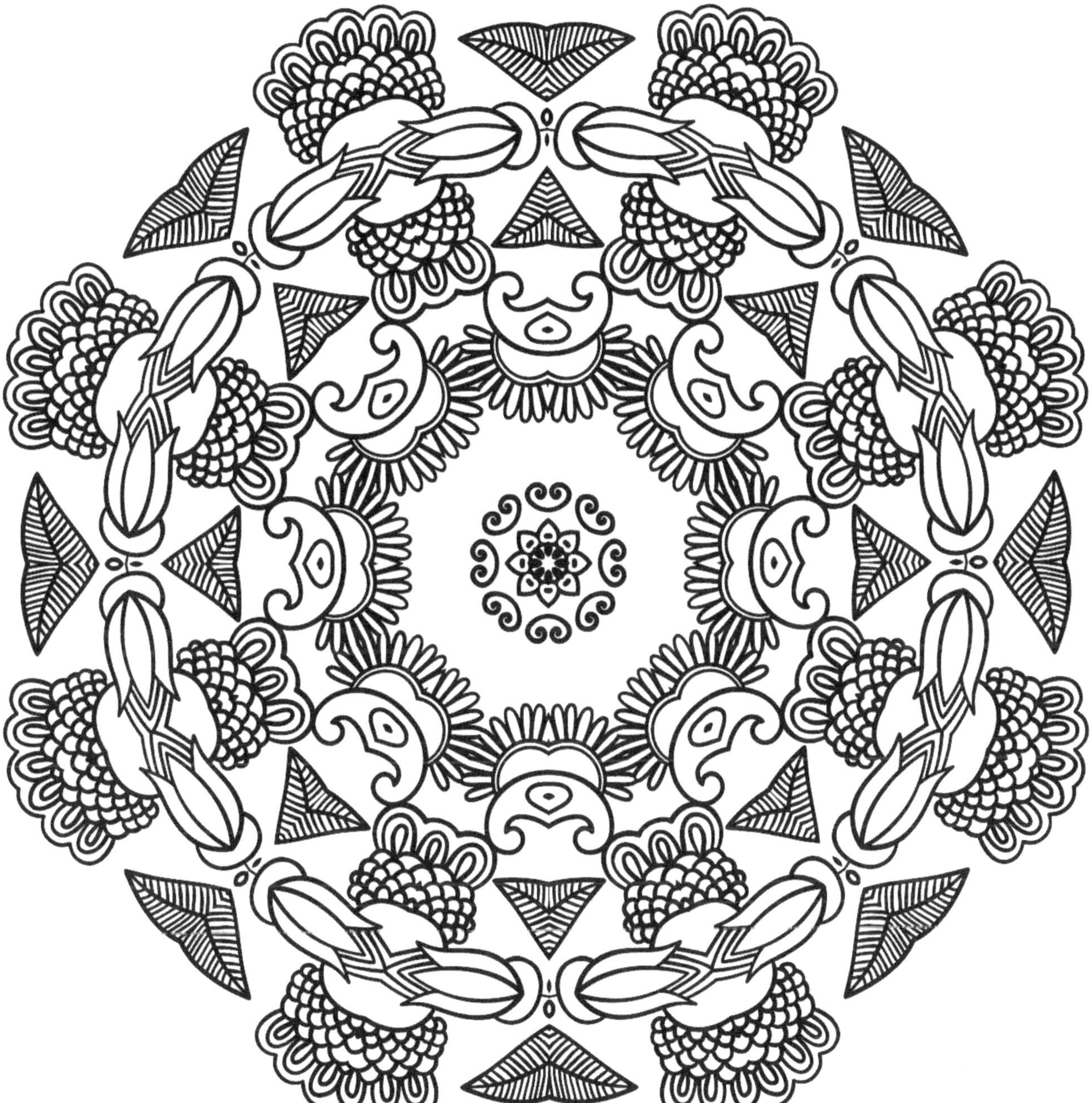

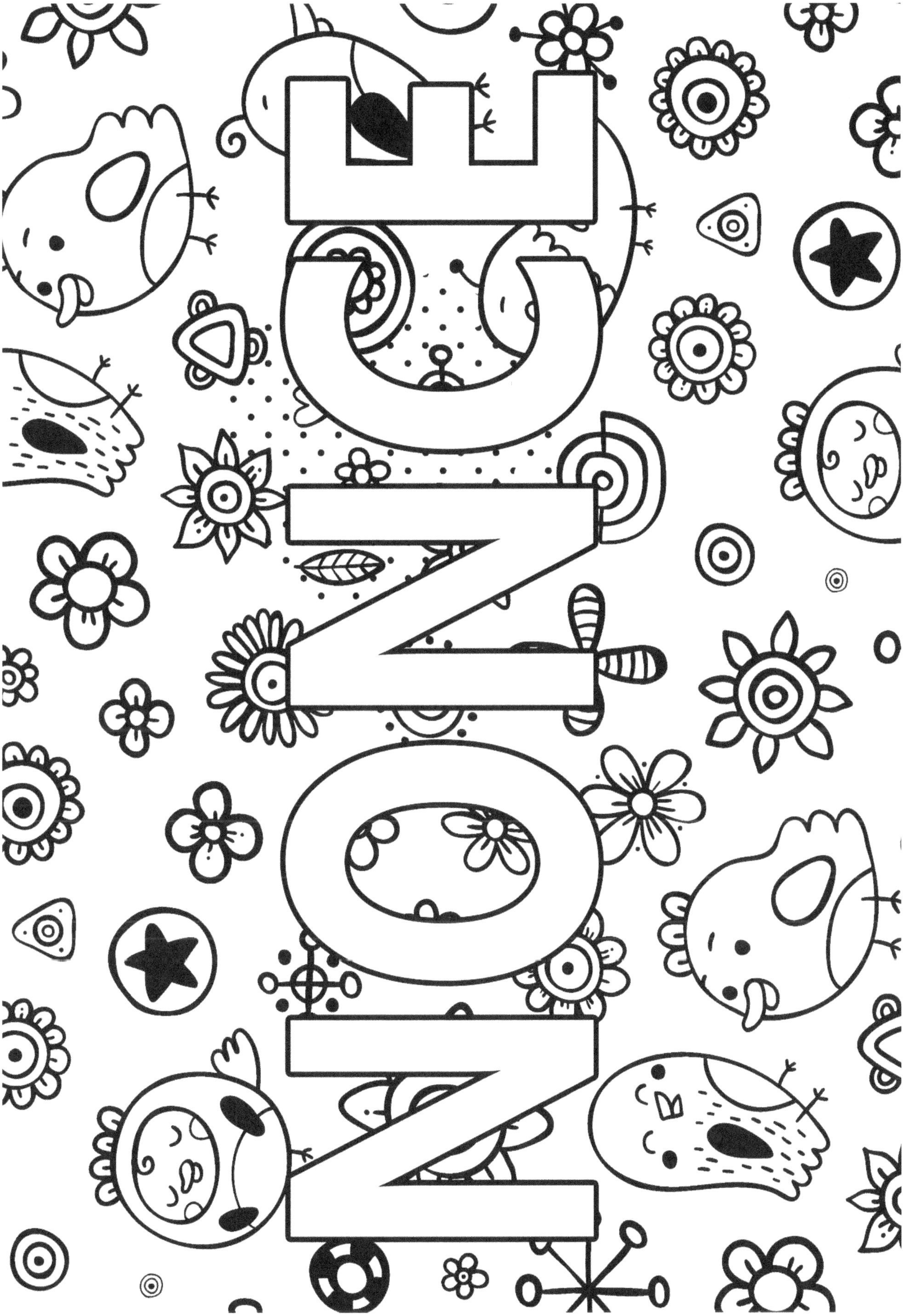
NONCE

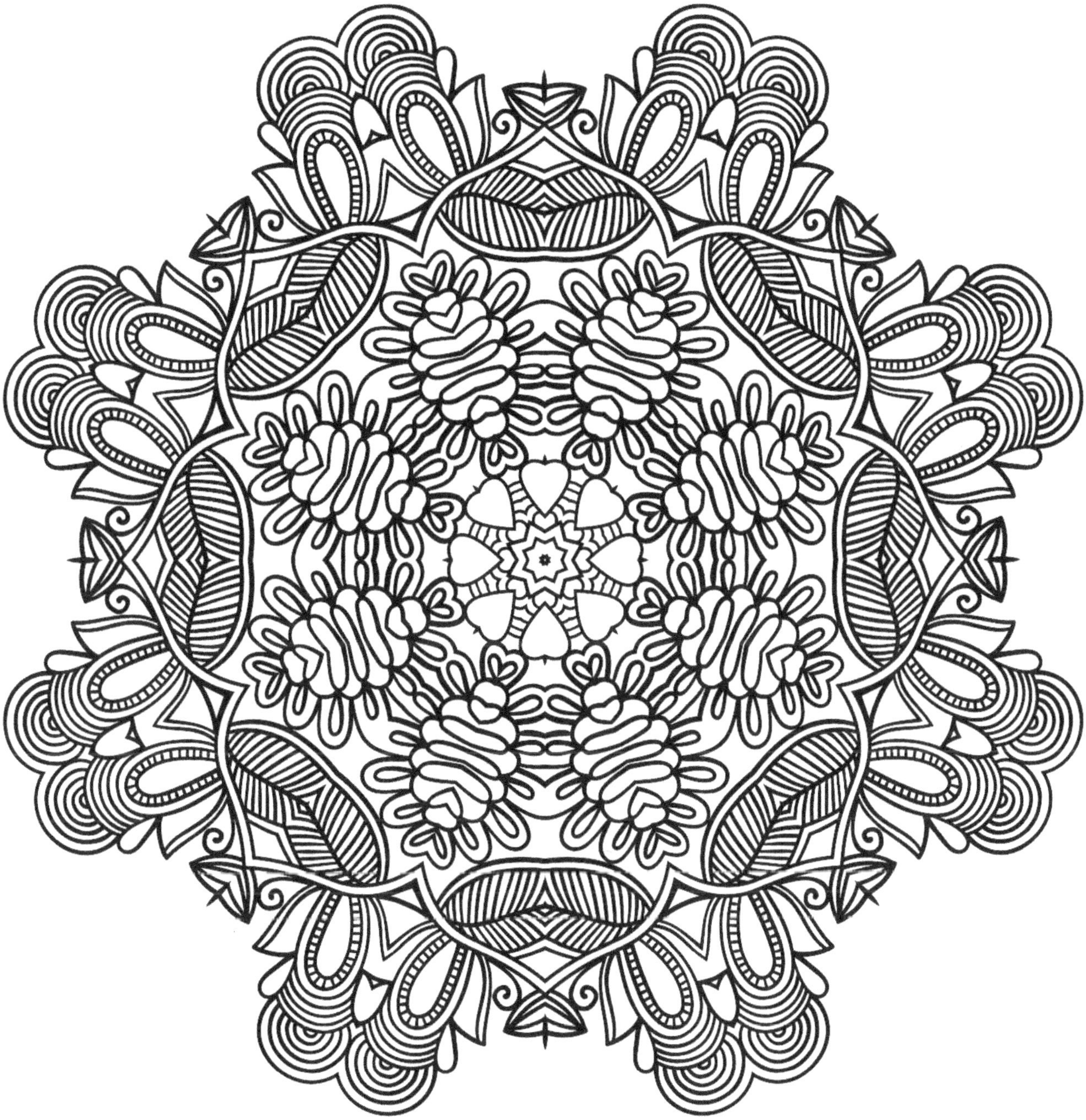

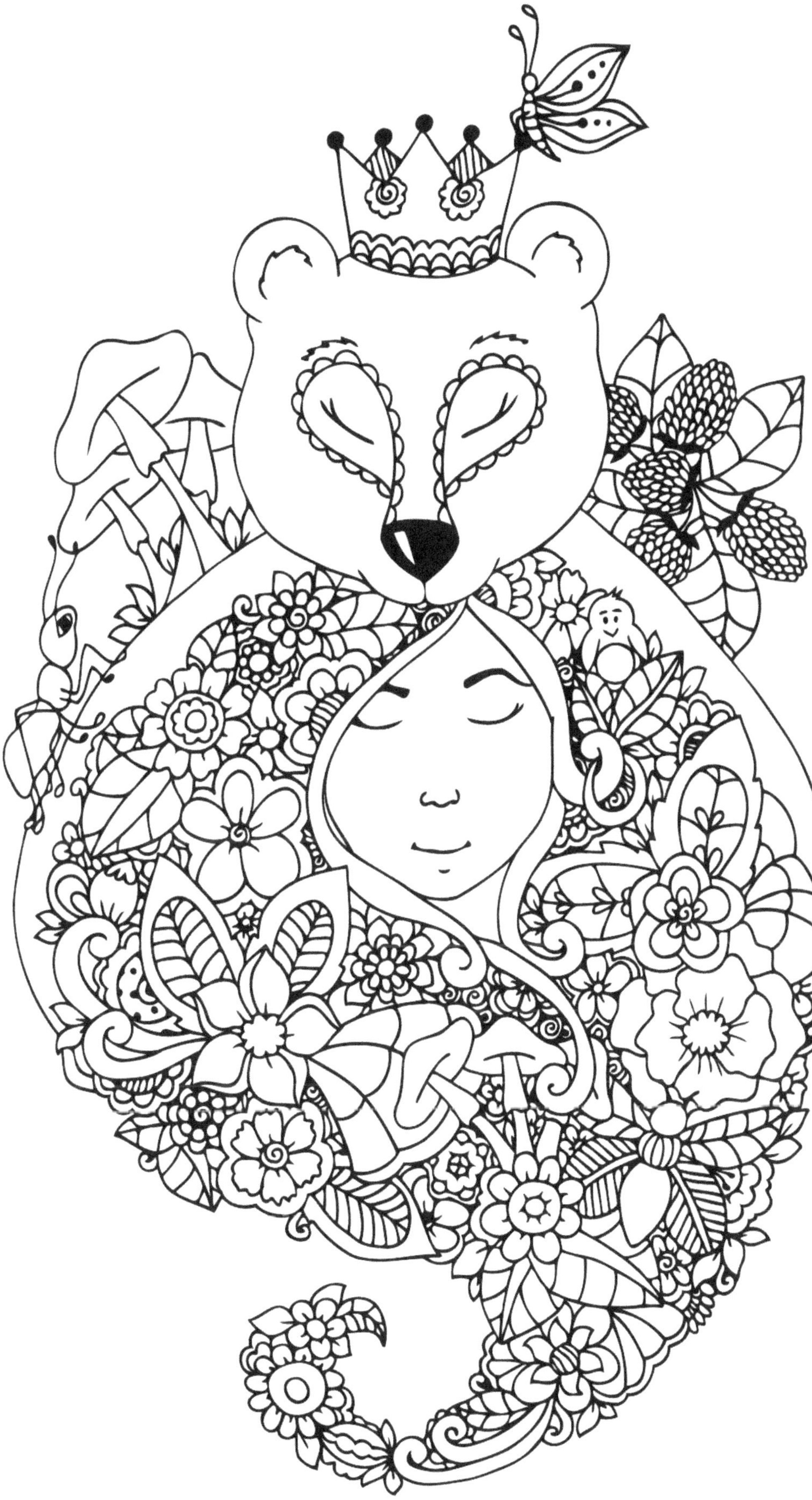

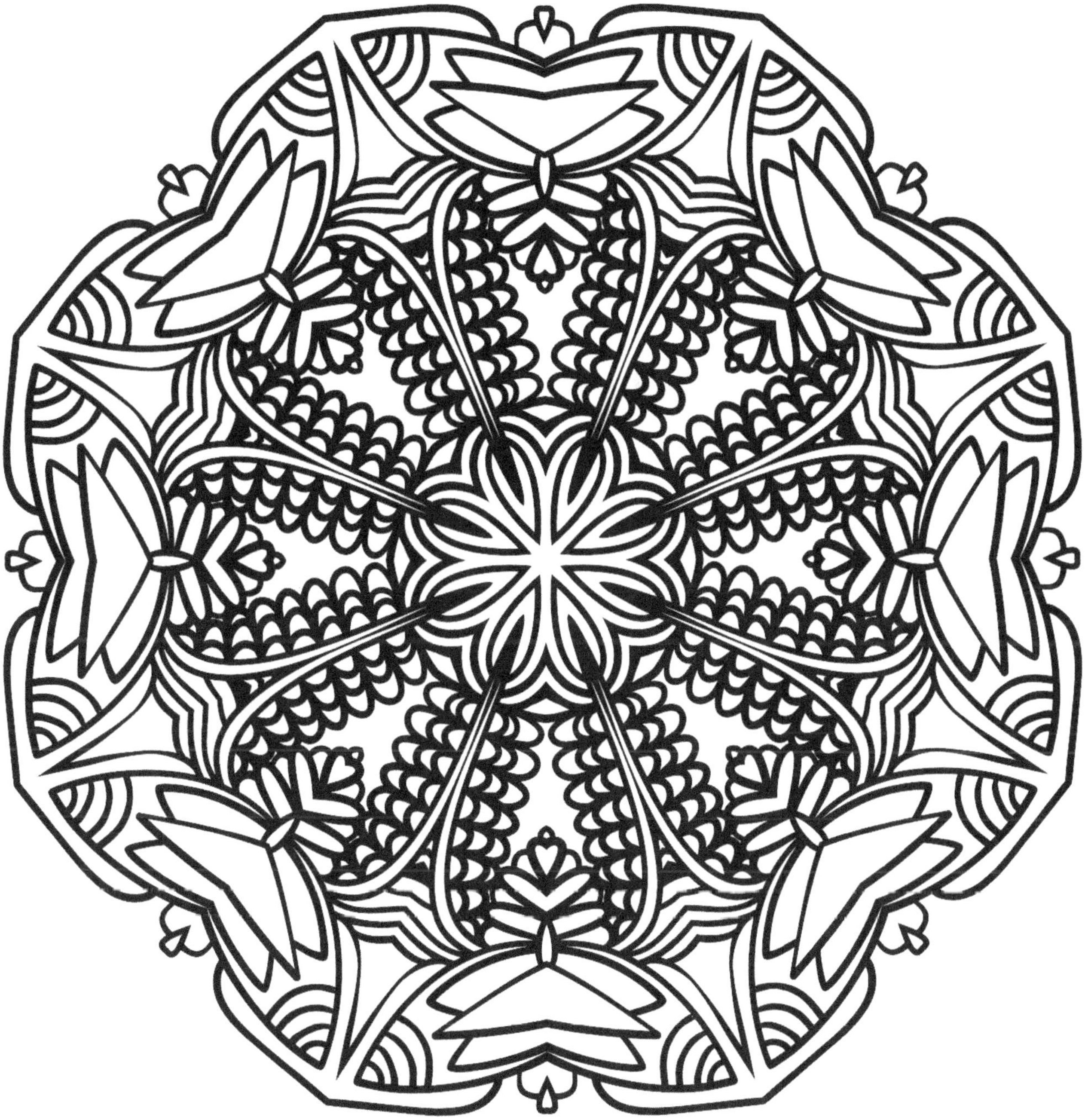

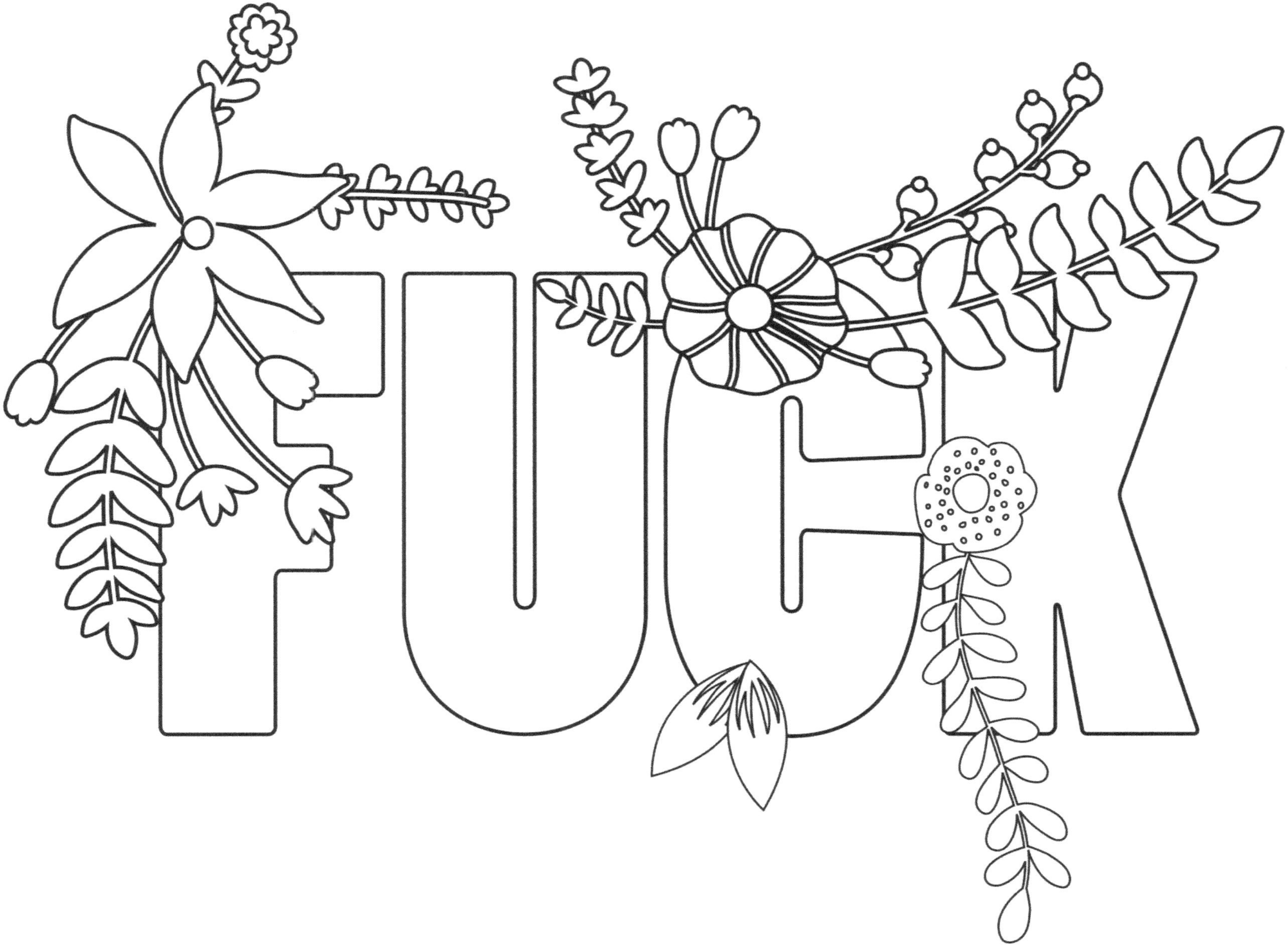
FUCK

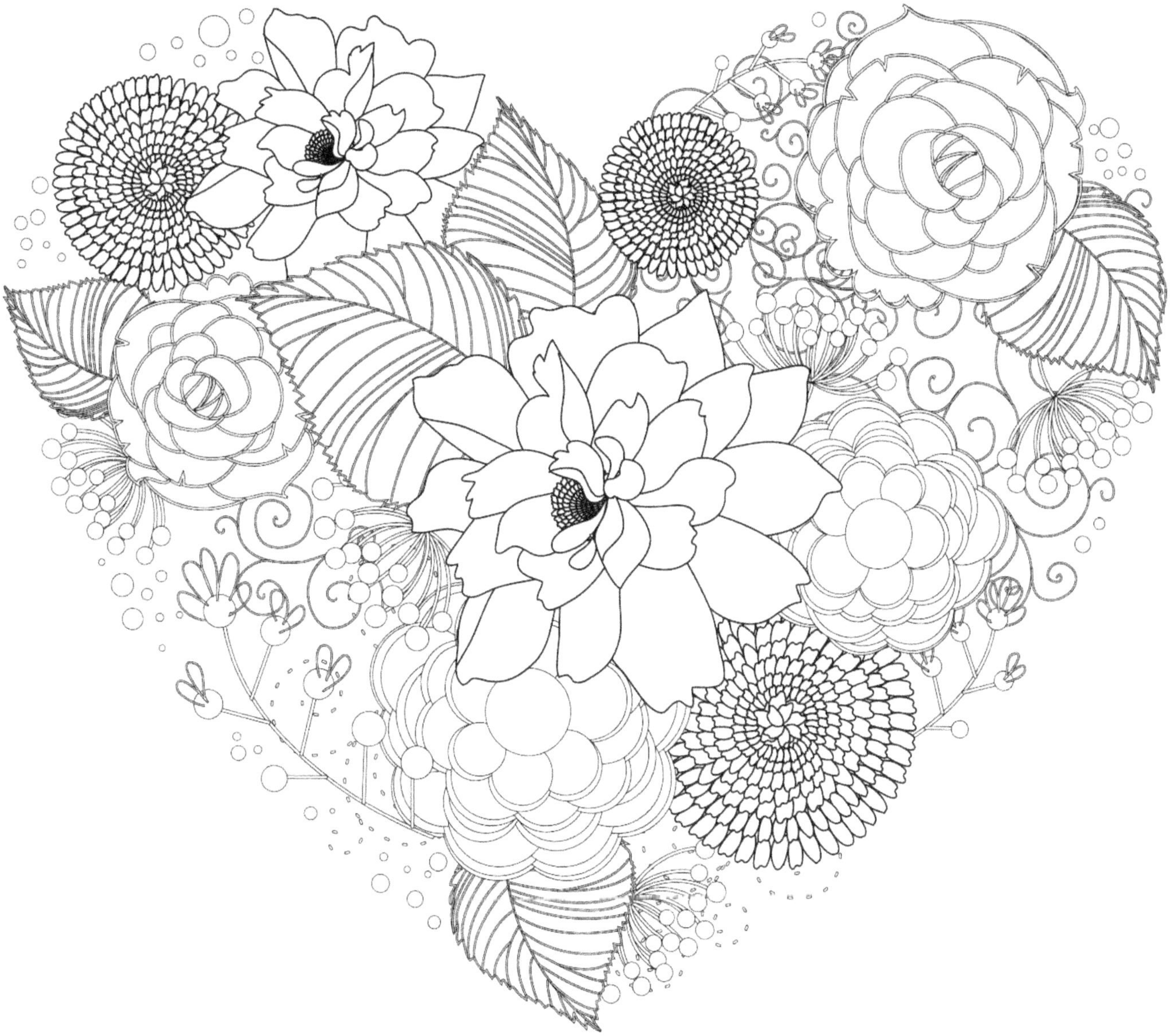

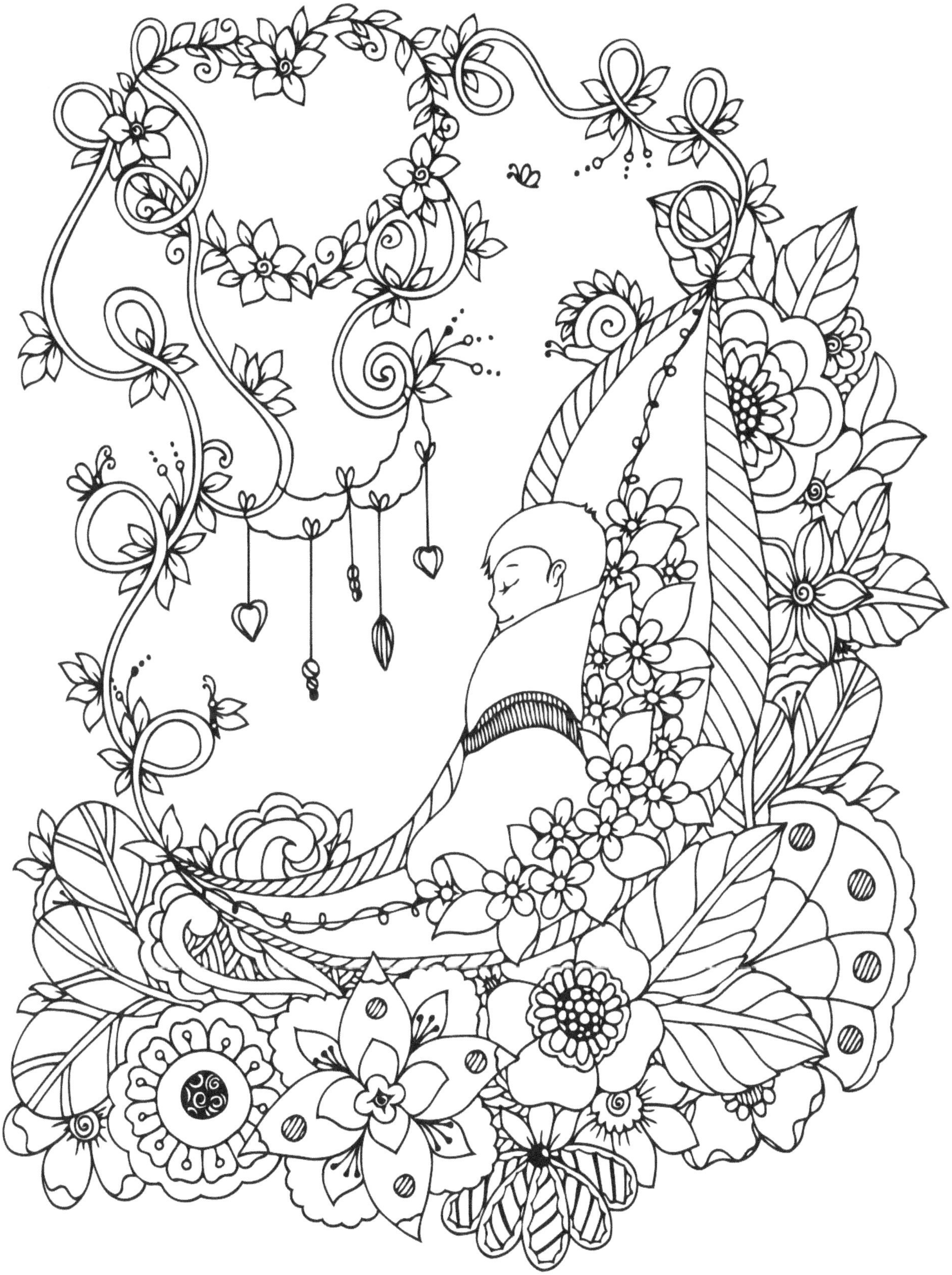

www.ingramcontent.com/pod-product-compliance
Lightning Source LLC
Chambersburg PA
CBHW081248180526
45170CB00007B/2346